# WIT, WISDOM, AND THE BUSINESS OF WEDDINGS

## ALAN BERG, CSP
### GLOBAL SPEAKING FELLOW

*Wit, Wisdom and the Business of Weddings*

Paperback ISBN: 9781081195724

Published by:
Wedding Business Solutions, LLC
& Left of Center Marketing & Publishing
Kendall Park, NJ © 2019

Acknowledgements:
Editor: Carole Berg
Book Design: Alan Berg & Amit Dey
Cover Design: Ian Berg

Written and Printed in the USA

# TABLE OF CONTENT

# DEDICATION

This book is dedicated to two, incredible women:

To My wife: Carole, you are my best friend, my soulmate and my co-pilot in love and life. Thank you for always being supportive of this crazy ride we're on, together.

To the memory of my mother: Mom, thank you for the positive attitude that you always exuded, and how you touched everyone around you with love and goodness. Your spirit lives on in all of us.

# PREFACE

I've been writing articles and blog posts for many, many years. My topics come from conversations I have with wedding pros, like you. When we talk at a conference, chat online, and collaborate during sales training and consultations, you give me ideas for the things that puzzle you, pain you and frustrate you. So, thank you for being the fuel for my fire.

This book is a compilation of some of my favorite subjects. It's not meant to be read front to back, although you're certainly welcome to do so. Rather, choose the topics that you need or want to know more about. Each chapter stands on its own. I've divided them into three categories: *Sales, Business* and *Inspiration*. If you've read any of my other books, or heard me present at a conference, or on a webinar, some of the concepts may sound familiar. That's good. Reinforcing, or confirming something you already know will make it a stronger part of your business processes. You may also find a little overlap between them, as I wrote each one at different times, and they weren't originally intended to be part of a book.

The *Sales* section covers topics from discount and negotiating, to pricing and objections, choices and ghosting (not getting replies to your emails and calls), to credit card fees and wedding shows. The *Business* section covers profitability and networking, to competition and social media. The *Inspiration* section covers a wide range of topics. In my speaking and writing, I strive to help you think differently and approach situations with a new, and hopefully clearer perspective. The topics here come from your experiences and mine. Many were sparked by epiphanies I've had in my personal life and business, and the stories you've shared with me.

While I certainly like writing about business and sales, I have to admit that I like writing about these life experiences the most. I'm often asked if I'm a 'motivational speaker.' While I hope that I'm motivational every time I present, for me, a motivational speaker delivers an inspirational message that's not usually heavy on content. You feel good after hearing it and it can certainly help your life, and business. However, it's not usually filled with the specifics and details you need to apply to your situation.

When I speak and write, I try to give you content, delivered in an inspirational and motivational way. Sure, to some of you that may sound like semantics. But for me, there's a clear distinction. If I'm asked to deliver a motivational keynote speech at a conference, I want you to feel good afterwards, but I also want you to walk away with some useful content. Even my book *"Your Attitude for Success,"* which is derived from a keynote speech, has usable content, in addition to being motivational. Unlike my other books, it doesn't focus on a particular topic (sales, websites or replying to digital inquiries). Its focus is to get you to take more and better actions, using stories of others who've already done so.

I've also purposely not included much information on websites in this book. I'm now working on a follow up to my first book, *"If your website was an employee, would you fire it?"*, where I'll dive deeper into things you should be doing to make your website convert better. Stay tuned for that one.

Whether you decide to read this book front to back, or skip around, I hope you enjoy it and get some ideas you can use, right away, in your business and life. Please share your stories of success and ideas for new articles and blog posts. Who knows, they may end up in a follow-up to this book! Thanks for taking this journey with me.

# SECTION I

# SALES

# 6 Steps to Wedding Show Success

**W**edding shows are still relevant for today's couples because they still like to see, hear, touch, smell and taste, before they buy. They're relevant for you because you crave the face-time and want to show the passion for what you do. Is there a magic formula for wedding show success? As with any other marketing vehicle you have to be an active participant. You can't just buy your booth and expect the sales to come rolling in. How can you make the most of your investment in wedding shows? First, think of it as more than just the day(s) of the show. Next, follow these 6 steps to maximize your return:

1. Before the show
   - Prepare your booth in advance and have a goal (sales, appointments, interested prospects, etc.).
   - Have them come to the show, specifically looking for you. Give your booth number and include visual elements that will tie your advance promotion to your actual booth.
   - Use Social Media, your website, direct mail, email, your voice mail and email auto-responder to alert your prospects that you'll be at the show.
   - Phone prospects who have shown interest and let them know you'll be at the show.

2. Prepare your follow up

- Don't wait until you get the list to decide what to do via phone, email and/or direct mail.

- Create the scripts, email templates and direct mail pieces before the show so you can get them out when the list arrives. Find out what data will be on the list and when you'll get it.

- Prepare a different follow up for those who scheduled appointments, those who showed interest and then the rest of the master list. The language should be different based upon what you do, or don't know about them and their level of interest.

3. At the show

- Make your booth stand out and reflect what you do. Don't distract or confuse them with elements that don't reflect what you do (i.e. photographers who use lots of flowers in their booth design).

- Use professional signage, something they can read from a distance with easy to read language and font styles.

- Put your signage up high so they can see it, so they can see it when you're booth is full of people.

- Don't sit down in your booth.

- Don't eat in your booth.

- Have a clear goal for the show. If you want to make appointments, have your appointment schedule with you. If you want to make sales, have contracts and a way to take deposits.

4. Staff your booth for the attendance

- Who you put in the booth makes a big difference. It isn't about just having enough bodies there. They have to be the right people, with the right skills.
- Teach them how to qualify quickly so you don't waste their or your time.
- Your business will be judged by the appearance of your booth and the attitude and professionalism of the staff.
- Using relatives and friends is fine... if they represent your brand well, have a good knowledge of your products, services and brand identity... and they can qualify, get the appointments and close some sales.

5. Follow up with your lists after the show
   - Be the first to follow up.
   - If you did number 2 correctly and prepared your follow up emails, phone scripts and/or direct mail, you'll be ready for this.
   - Use similar branding, colors, fonts and offers as you do in your booth and your other marketing.
   - Include photos and similar visuals from your booth in your follow-up to tie them to your look and feel at the show.
   - Leave compelling voice messages that refer to the email and/or direct mail you send them.

6. Follow up again based upon the wedding date
   - The residual effects of the show don't end the day of the show. Pay attention to their wedding dates and market to them accordingly.

- What's the right timing? There is none, but you should have a pretty good idea when most people book you compared to their wedding dates.
- When should you stop following up? When you want to start profiting from the show. Each couple books their wedding services on their own schedule.

Remember that it's your job to measure your return on investment (ROI), so have a plan as to how you're going to do that. Many, if not most of the sales you make will be after the show, so have a way to connect those dots so you'll know whether the ROI justifies reserving your booth for the next show.

# *S*

# Auto-Replies Oughta Go!

Auto-responders. Out of Office messages. We get them every day. Some of us send them every day. Are they providing a good experience to the recipient? Does the person receiving these messages feel better about the interaction? Do any of us really need another email in our inbox?

I speak and consult with countless wedding and event pros each year and I know that many of you like your auto-responders. You have them set up to reply to inquiries. You have them set up to reply whether you're in the office or out. So, let's turn the tables on you and see what experience you're actually providing. When you're the customer and you email a company you've never done business with, and you get an almost immediate reply that says something like: *"Your message is very important to us. We'll get back to you as soon as we can."* How does that make you feel? Do you feel like they've actually responded? Or, is it just a validation that their computer has received your email?

## Where's the value?

My simple philosophy on auto-responders or out of office messages is that they should add value to the recipient. Telling me that you've received my message adds no value for me. Saying that you'll get back to me as soon as you can is a statement of the obvious. I hope you'd get back to me as soon as you can and not make me wait any longer than necessary.

What I'm looking for is valuable information that wasn't on your website, and therefore I didn't have before I sent you my email, or filled out your contact form. I only use an out of office reply when I'm out of my office for a full day, or longer. It states when I'll be out, where I'll be, gives information on my availability and how to get a message to me when it's urgent, including my cell phone number. I've seen way too many messages that say to call for more information or faster service, and they don't include the phone number. It also includes my full email signature with all of the included contact information.

### Are you listening?

What about auto-responders that send information to whoever completes your contact form? Unless your system is sophisticated enough to only send what they asked for, and nothing more, then I'm not a fan. In my presentations and articles, I've often said not to answer questions they haven't yet asked, and don't send information they didn't request. Your marketing materials can't qualify or close a prospect, only you can. They're already interested or they wouldn't have made the inquiry. Show them that your company provides real, personalized customer service by actually replying, instead of reactively sending the same information to everyone, regardless of their need.

### The good, the bad and the ugly

When I send out emails to my contact list I get dozens upon dozens of auto-responders and out of office messages. I've been saving them up to use for an article or post, just like this one. Here's some of what I've gotten from real wedding and event pros, along with my thoughts on each:

*"We will respond very soon."*

— that's all it said. My thought on how to improve this is to get rid of it altogether. It serves no purpose and adds no value.

*"Thank you for your interest in XYZ Properties. One of our coordinators will be contacting you shortly. If you would like to view our facilities please feel free to stop by anytime Mon.- Wed. from 10am - 6pm or Thurs.- Sat. from 10am - 3pm. Thank you again and have a great day!"*

— I like that they include their hours, but how about including their address and phone number?

*"Greetings,*

*Due to high workload, we are currently checking and responding to email M-F twice daily at 12n and 4p. Thank you for understanding this move to more efficiency and effectiveness. It helps us accomplish more to serve you better."*

— This one always bristles me as I'm wondering that if I email at 4:05pm I won't hear back until at least after 12 noon the next day. They'd be better off not saying anything and just responding when they can. Trying to be more efficient and checking your email twice a day is fine, just don't telegraph to prospects that it will be hours until they may get a reply. Customers don't care how much you accomplish, unless it's their job you're working on.

*"This email address no longer being monitored. Your email is not being forwarded and will not be answered."*

— if you can put on an auto-responder why can't you just forward the email to the new email address? What if a past customer refers someone to them and gives out the only email address they had for you? Don't you want the inquiry? Why wouldn't you at least include the new email address? To me this screams: *"Go away, we don't want to do business with you."*

*"Thanks for emailing us! We will respond to your email within 3 business days."*

— 3 business days?? Are you kidding me? I don't think I would want to do business with a company that is telling me that it may take 3 days for them to reply. I travel more than most people and I'm almost always able to reply by the next day, even when I'm out of the country. I pride myself on replying as quickly as I can, so this one really bothers me.

*"I'm on Vacation and will be off the grid!!*

*Any emergencies or if you wish to make a wedding payment*

*You can phone the store and ask for Mary the bookeeper.*

*Thanks and Happy Planning"*

— while I applaud her for taking some time off, telling me to phone the store without putting the phone number, or Mary's email, is inconvenient (oh, and book-keeper is misspelled).

*"Hi there - thanks for your email!*

*After watching me plan so many wonderful trips for my happy clients - my hubby started to get a little jealous - so we decided to finally take a vacation ourselves! I will be out of the office from Sat April 26 to Mon May 5th sailing the warm waters of the Caribbean!*

*I will have limited access to email/voicemail but my wonderful colleague Susan Smith will be here if there is something that cannot wait until the 5th! Her information is below.*

*[Susan's contact info was here]*

*Thanks - have a great week!*

*[this was followed by her name and contact info]*

— I love the conversational voice here and the fact that she gives you not only the info, but also the contact info for the person who is covering for her. This is adding value.

## Our lesson for today...

I'm sorry if it sounds like I'm up on my soapbox a little here, but I know that I'm just voicing a common opinion I hear, all the time, from wedding and event pros, like you. My rule of thumb when marketing is simple: *"If you don't like something you see, or experience when you're the customer, don't do that to your customers and prospects"*. So, unless you yell "goody" every time you get an auto-responder, think twice about subjecting your prospects and customers to them. Ask yourself what you would want to happen if you were the customer. You'd probably just want a real person to get back to you as quickly as they can. That's what's expected, so you don't have to send me that info.

## Thoughts and Ideas

## Do you accept credit cards?

That seems to be a strange question these days, but it's a common one that pops up on forums and in social media groups. With the cost of transactions ranging from just over 1% to as high as 4% (or more with additional fees) it's certainly a subject worth talking about. It's a cost of doing business, but can you, or should you try to mitigate that cost?

I think it's as much a mindset as a real cost. In an article: *"You can't save your way to prosperity,"* I talked about cost-saving strategies and how most are misguided. There's a limit to how much you can save. You have to have electricity, gas for your truck, supplies, payroll and taxes. No matter how hard you try, you can't reduce your costs to zero. Are the efforts worth the savings? Over time the savings will add up, but I contend that a better use of most of our time is in making more dollars, rather than trying to save pennies.

### Let's do the math

A while back I was consulting with a wedding pro and he was lamenting about how it costs him 4% when he receives funds through his website. If he does $100,000 in collections, that's costing him $4,000 per year in credit card fees. If he does $200,000 in collections through credit/debit cards, it costs him $8,000 per year. The only way to reduce that to zero is to stop accepting credit cards. These days that's also likely to limit your sales as some people only want to pay with their credit or debit card. You also get the funds now, as opposed to waiting for a check or cash, as you can accept the cards remotely, but cash would be in person and checks are becoming a much rarer form of commerce for today's generation of wedding couples.

Back to my client; I asked him how many of his customers he might have lost if he didn't take credit cards, and while it's hard to say, it's likely he would have lost a few. The most he can save is $4,000, or $8,000, depending upon his collections. It's very likely that the lost sales would have cost him more than the credit card fees are costing.

## A different approach

We both agreed that telling the customer they have to pay the credit card fees on top of their purchase wasn't a good idea. None of us likes that when we're the customer. So, I asked him a different question. Assuming an average sale of $1,000 (for ease of discussion), how many of his customers would have balked and not bought if his price had been $1,050? In other words, if he had raised his rate by 5%, would any of his customers have said No? He thought about it and said that he felt all of his customers still would have bought. What about $1,100? He said they all still would have bought. So I told him to immediately raise his rate to $1,100 and stop worrying about the 4% because he's now covering the fee and making more on top of that. And that extra is all profit (after taxes, of course).

## Change your mindset

The approach I take for my business is to assume that all of my collections will be via credit/debit card. I also put a number of 5%

on that when I'm doing my projections and budgeting. I know that I'll get checks and cash from some clients and that my actual processing costs less than 5%, so the real number will be lower. But if I estimate at 5%, when someone pays me with check or cash I look at it as making 5%, as opposed to looking at credit card transactions as costing me 5%. It's a mindset shift. I'd rather look at profits than costs.

## Is saving bad?

Should he look for a better deal on credit card processing? Sure. He's recently signed up for Square and can use their invoicing feature, as well as the device on his phone for mobile payments. A better use of his time is marketing, networking, evaluating his pricing strategy and pricing power, and working to increase his average sale. The amount you can save is always limited to what you spend. The amount you can make is unlimited. And you don't want to save your way to oblivion. If you stop marketing and reign in your expenses too much you're likely to hurt your business' potential earnings. I've said it many times, but you have to invest in your business first if you want others to invest in you.

## Thoughts and Ideas

# Don't blow today's sale
## for a bigger one

While presenting at an industry event, I asked the group to let me know if anyone gets a new lead, while we were meeting. A little while later, one attendee told me a new lead had just come through, via email. It was from a university, but a department with which he had never worked. It sounded like a referral, although they didn't mention that in their email. As he read us all the email, it seemed to me as though they weren't shopping around, rather they were checking availability and pricing.

**Make their job easier**

I asked if the message included the title of the person who sent the email, and he said she was an Executive Assistant. I suggested that, to me, it seemed as though this probably just got dropped in her lap, and the easier he makes it for her, the faster he'll get the sale. He expressed that he'd like to get her on the phone, to discuss the details of the event. I told him that she hadn't asked for a call, and if we were right, and she had been referred by another department, with which he's already worked, and she wasn't shopping around, that he should reply to her email with a quote. Just summarize what he suggested would be best for her event, based upon what she had sent, give her the price, and ask if he should reserve that for her.

He hesitated, and said that he'd still like to get her on the phone first. I asked why, and he said: "I'd like to see..." and I stopped him. I said that he was using the word "I" too much. It wasn't what he wanted that mattered. It's what she wants. I again suggested that he send the quote and ask for the sale. He hesitated again.

## What about Top-Down Selling?

While I advocate a Top Down approach to selling, in this case it would be better to lock up the sale that you're being given (not quite on a silver platter, but close), and then try to upsell them, later. With Top-Down Selling you try to get the bigger sale today, and then take things away to work down to a lower price if they object. While I usually prefer that you do that, I don't want to lose the sale that's in front of you, on the possibility that they might buy more. I was suggesting that he quote her the best option, based upon what she had asked. That's still a form of Top-Down Selling. Had he been able to have a conversation with her, he may have been able to quote a bigger package. However, there was something about what and how she had written that gave me the feeling that we should take the easy sale today, and then suggest the upsell later. Maybe it's my experience, or Spidey-sense tingling, but my gut said to go for the close.

Eventually, he relented and tried it my way. A little while later, he reported that he had closed the sale. Given the lead-time that we usually have for events, be it days, weeks, months, or more, there's usually ample time to go for the upsell. According to the WeddingWire Newlywed Report, 74% of couples go over their budgets (I know, you're shocked!). That means that some people, who had been trying to stick to their budget when they hired you, have subsequently gone over their budget, and might be more willing to add some of the products and services they previously passed on. The only way you'll know, is if you ask them.

## When should you ask for the upsell?

It's likely that you have many points of contact with your clients, after the initial sale, and before their event. Some are via email, some on the phone/Skype/Facetime and some may be in person. Those conversations are a great time to ask good questions, listen for their answers, and suggest upsells that help them have the outcomes that they need and want.

## Would it make sense?

In my sales book "Shut Up and Sell More Weddings & Events," I mention a great way to make these suggestions (recommended by my friend Lois Creamer). Start the sentence with: *"Would it make sense...?"* For example: *"Would it make sense to add the pasta station?"* or *"Would it make sense to create a really unique groom's cake?"* or *"Would it make sense to add the custom monogram?"* or *"I know that you didn't initially go with the photobooth, but we still have one available for your wedding date. Would it make sense to give your guests the great fun and keepsakes to remember their experience?"* You see, you can ask for almost any upsell with this method. It puts the decision back on them, and feels less "salesy" than *"Would you like to buy...?"* Ceci Johnson, who designs amazing, high-end invitations, uses a phrase with the same suggestive approach: *"What if...?"* as in: *"What if we _____ (and she suggest something the customer hadn't already asked for?"*

## Bird-in-the-hand, or Top-Down?

Each situation will be different, so you need to be looking for the buying signals. Unless what they're looking for today won't give them the outcomes they want (in which case, you shouldn't take the sale), it's sometimes best to take the sale they're giving you today. Nurture that bird-in-hand sale and suggest the upsells later. If you confuse them with more choices now, they may reply with *"we need to think about it"*, instead of buying today. Our job is to reduce their choices, not increase them. If they're ready to buy today, help them do that. Don't get greedy and push them for the bigger sale.

# *S*

## Friday and Sunday Pricing – Should It Be Lower?

I often see heated discussions on social media about whether you should charge the same for Friday, Sunday, weekday, and off-season weddings and events, as you do for Saturday nights. There are passionate arguments on both sides. Some people contend that you're doing the same work, therefore you should charge the same. That's a sound platform. Others say that they're only going to do a limited number of events per year, therefore they charge the same regardless of the month or day, also a sound argument.

The other side speaks of not getting as many inquiries for Fridays, Sundays, or weekday events—so they offer a discount to encourage those to book. That too is a sound platform. There are successful businesses on both sides of this discussion.

### So what's the right answer?

That's the thing—there is no one right or wrong answer. It's going to depend upon your business model and aspirations. Are you trying to increase the number of events you do? If you're already booking the most popular dates you can't do any more events unless you take on more staff, something many of you are reluctant to do. Trying to book the dates that are less in demand isn't as easy as just saying you're available. It takes a strategy that includes marketing, advertising, networking and yes, pricing. I'm not saying you *have* to discount to book those dates, but it has to be part of the discussion.

## Supply and Demand

The most basic principle of economics is supply and demand. I've spoken and written about this often, and it's a common discussion when I'm consulting with businesses, like yours. What we all want is more people wanting to buy our product or service (that's the demand) than we have available to sell (that's our supply or inventory). Then we have pricing power. When there's less demand there's pressure to lower pricing.

## What's your inventory?

All of us have an inventory, and it's not just the physical goods that are involved in our work. Time is the most limited resource of all. No matter how many weddings or events you can do in a day, there is a limit. Even if you staff-up you're going to eventually run into a wall and run out of supply. For some of us it's easier than for others. An entertainment company can hire another DJ easier than a venue can build another banquet room. If you're doing the right marketing and networking you should be getting enough leads to at least book the most popular dates in your market. If you can fill your calendar early in the season or without much price resistance, you probably have pricing power.

## Do you like getting a discount?

Another factor to consider is that everyone likes getting a discount, don't you? Have you ever asked for a discount? Probably. If so then don't fault your customers for asking you for one. You don't always get one when you ask and you don't have to give one just because you've been asked. Please don't get upset or insulted because someone has asked you for a discount. You don't have to say, "Yes." You can say no, with a smile... and then ask for the sale!

## But my services are the same no matter the day

That's true. You're going to provide the same level of quality and service no matter what you're being paid, no matter the day of the week, or month of the year. That said, there are lots of times when we get to pay more, or less, based upon some factor. Movie theaters often have weekday matinee pricing, yet the movie is exactly the same. Seniors and students are often offered discounts to the same events that the rest of us pay full price. Military families are often offered discounts as well. Is it right, or wrong, for any of these groups to pay less than everyone else?

## Discounting vs. negotiating

In another chapter of this book I discuss discounting versus negotiating. The examples above were all discounts that have a structure. They have rules and those rules are applied the same to everyone. Every senior who attends the show, or stays at the same hotel, is offered the exact same discount. If they ask for a bigger discount the answer will be 'No'. The rules for the discount can be easily explained and you can see whether you qualify or not.

Offering a discount for a Friday evening wedding versus a Saturday evening wedding is an easy rule. If Saturdays book up fast for you, and Fridays don't, you might choose to offer an incentive. Or you could just have a higher price for Saturday, not a lower one for Friday. Yes, it's semantics, but that too is very common. Workers get paid time and a half for overtime, yet they're doing the same work. Hotels and airlines charge more for high-demand times.

## The Wild West

Negotiating, on the other hand, has no rules. You give bigger or smaller discounts to different customers, even when they're buying the very same thing. You offer larger or smaller discounts depending upon how badly you want that sale, or in many cases, how desperate you are for that sale. I've often said you should always negotiate as if you don't need the business—even when you do! In this digitally connected world people talk, and read, what others have gotten.

## Should you discount Fridays, Sundays, and weekdays?

Whether you decide to discount—or not, or charge more for some dates—or not, is solely up to you. You should do it to fulfill your business needs and goals, not anyone else's. Listen to what others are doing, but don't copy them.  Do what's right for you. As a consultant, I help people decide what's right for each client. As a businessman, I don't expect anyone else to copy what I do, because that's what's right for me and it might not be right for you. Choose your own right path.

# I'M A HYPOCRITE, ARE YOU?

Every so often, I'm guilty of buying based upon price. There, I said it. But, that makes me a hypocrite. I want my customers choosing me as their speaker, mastermind leader, consultant or for a website review, not because I'm the cheapest price. Rather, I want you choosing me because you feel, for that particular need, that the value you'll get, exceeds the cost. If the return on your investment, exceeds the cost of the investment, then it's probably a good choice. However, not all 'returns' are the same, and not all investments are the same.

I recently shopped around for home and auto insurance. The thing is, I like my current company. They have great customer service, and, in the times we've had to make claims, the service has been wonderful. So, why did I shop around? I got another increase in rate, and when I looked back, I had been increased every 6 months (on the auto) and every year (on the home). I wasn't looking to make a change. I was looking for verification that my rate was still fair and competitive. I don't need them to have the lowest rate, when their service is so good. But, I do need them to be somewhere in the same ballpark as other, high-quality companies.

## Let the search begin

So, I requested quotes from other, well-known companies. I requested quotes through different affiliations (AAA, Costco, etc.). I contacted the companies that do a lot of TV advertising, promising to save you significant sums over your current company. Most of the quotes that I got were similar to what I was paying. Maybe a little more. Maybe a little less. That was reassuring, although I was a little disappointed I didn't get a lower quote. I was also disappointed that, when I emailed my current agent, no one got back to me.

Then something interesting happened. I got a quote through AAA, one of my affiliations, that was significantly lower than the others I had received. At first, I thought it must be a mistake. Maybe it was a 6-month rate, instead of a year. So, I sent the agent my current policies, and asked him to please check, line by line, and tell me what the differences were. All major line items were the same, or better, on both the home and auto. It was a 45% savings on both the home and auto policies. I don't mind paying a little more, but I can't see paying almost double.

## Double down, or fold?

So, why would someone pay double, or even more, for your service, or mine? The difference is in the perceived value. For auto and home insurance, you're hoping to never need to use the service. It's kind of funny when you think about it, but we pay in every year and hope that we never need to collect. That's especially true of life insurance! You don't tend to find out how good they are, until you need to contact them or make a claim.

For your service, or mine, people are going to start to see the value, from the first time they interact with you, your marketing, or your website. They're buying something they want, or need, and it usually affects more than just them. For weddings and events, people buy outcomes, not processes. They want great food, but most don't care how you make it. They want a fantastic video, but most don't care how you shoot or edit it. They want beautiful flowers, dresses, invitations, jewelry, and more. But most aren't interested in the process, just the end result.

## Looks the same to me

I was OK spending a lot less for my home and auto insurance, because I believe that the new company will be there if I need to make a claim; will continue with friendly customer service (as they have, so far); and that they will live up to the terms of the policy. If they had been nasty, or indifferent, in my dealings with the agent, I wouldn't have made the switch. I even had to call the customer service line, with a question, and the woman who answered was extremely friendly and helpful, validating my decision.

I've said this many times before; if you can't perceive any difference between companies, the lower price will win. It's not whether there actually is a difference. It's whether you can perceive one. It's the same for your couples; if they can't perceive any difference between what you're providing and another company; and if they also like them, trust them and believe they'll deliver an acceptable outcome, then a lower price, or better responsiveness, or better customer experience, will win.

## Do unto others

So, I'm really not a hypocrite, at least not in this case. I shopped exactly the same way I would expect others to shop for me. I'm competing with people who will speak for a lot less, or even free. Some of those people do a decent job. Some may even do a very good job. But, if my client can't see any difference between having me speak, consult or do sales training, versus anyone else, then the lower price will win. Everything I do, from my presentations to my website, from my professionally-designed marketing to the way I interact and communicate, is designed to show what's different about choosing me.

What are you doing to differentiate yourself from your competitors, other than price? Are you making important business decisions based upon price? Are you choosing the cheapest printing for your marketing, or are you hiring a professional graphic designer? Did you make your website yourself, or did you hire a pro? Are you looking for every free way to promote yourself, or are you investing in the best placement, on the best sites? I'll tell you what I tell my clients; invest more in yourself and your business, if you want others to invest more in you.

# S

# I OBJECT! OBJECTION OVERRULED!

One of the most misunderstood parts of the sales process is objections. Those of you who are not natural sales people hate objections. You see them as road blocks to getting the sale. I'm here to ask you to see them differently. If they tell you what they want, you give them a price, and you make the sale without them presenting any objections... you didn't make a sale, you took an order. There was no selling involved. This is what happens in most retail stores these days. You go and pick out what you want and pay for it at the register. There's no selling involved. There may be a bit of merchandising, to get you to find the items that they want you to buy, but unless someone helped you buy something other than what you came in looking for, there was no selling involved.

## Objections are buying signals and opportunities

However, if you go through your sales pitch (and whether you should have a set sales pitch or not is a subject for another day), you give them the price, and they voice an objection, a question, a "what if..." or a "but...", that's when the selling starts. Objections are buying signals and opportunities. If they weren't interested, they wouldn't bother asking the question, or voice the objection. When they say "what if...." Or "but...", they're really saying "I'll be closer to buying if you answer this well". It's really just a mindset shift to see these as opportunities. If they weren't interested, you never would have gotten the inquiry. If they aren't still interested they will either stop replying, or leave – if you're meeting with them in person.

Even price objections are buying signals. They're signaling that if you can show them the value, or another option, they might buy. Again, if they weren't interested at all, the sales process would just stop. But it isn't stopping, they're hanging in there with you. I'm not saying you need to lower your price to get the sale. I've done many webinars and live presentations about value, so please don't lower your price without getting something of value back in return. Every dollar you discount without getting anything in return, is profit you gave away!

## Agree when they disagree

One of the best ways to diffuse an objection is to agree with them. If you've tried to close the sale and couldn't, and they say *"We want to go home and think about it."*, you can say *"Of course you do. I wouldn't expect you to make such an important decision at our first meeting"*. However, if you hear this often: *"You've given us so much to think about, we need to go home and process it."*, and that's why you don't close many sales on the first appointment... that's your fault, not theirs. Your job is to help them reduce the choices down to only the most appropriate, not confuse them with everything you offer. No one needs everything you offer, so listen first, then pitch them.

## Feel – Felt – Found

One of the best ways to handle most objections is with a process that I heard many, many years ago. I've tried to find the origin of it, but even Google can't help me. If you do a Google search for *"Feel – Felt – Found"* you'll get over 2 million results, but none that I've seen give the original source. It's so simple, yet so effective. There are 3 parts to this:

**Feel** – empathize with their situation: *"I understand how you feel."*

**Felt** – show them that others, just like them, have had this same thought.

**Found** – is what you wanted to say to overcome the objection, but doing that right away would be more confrontational.

## Here's how this works with real objections (hint – it works really well)

Objection: *"You're the first one we've seen. We need to look around."*

Response: *"I understand how you feel. Many other couples we've seen have felt the same way, that they need to do an endless search. What they found is that they, like you, have already done a lot of the research online, and you know what you want before you get here. So once you find it, you buy it, even if it's the first place you've been. Why keep looking when your must-have list is covered? And that's why so many buy from us on their first appointment."*

Objection: *"That's more than we wanted to spend."*

Response: *"I totally understand how you feel and I know how things add up for weddings. I had a couple in last week who felt the same way. They found that there were things they hadn't thought of when they made their budget, and there are other places they can try to save, and they went with us because they didn't want to look back after their wedding and think they skimped on their _____ (fill in what you do)."*

There are countless ways to use Feel – Felt – Found, without using those specific words. I want to give you a foundation for coming up with your own wording, phrasing you'll feel comfortable using in real sales appointments. Play around with this and you'll find that it's almost magical how well it works. It's a much softer, more comfortable process for both you, and your couples.

## ~~If~~ When they come back

When your customers go looking around, and come back to you with: *"We found a lower price with another vendor."* – what they are really saying is: *"We want to book with you, but this lower price is making us confused."* Think about it, if they had found everything they want, and need, including a lower price, why didn't they book that other vendor? It's because they really want you to do their wedding. You don't have to match the price to get the sale. You have to remind them of the value of choosing you, over anyone else. You can certainly use Feel – Felt – Found here: *"I understand how you feel, and thanks for coming back. I had a couple in the other day who had also looked around and got a lower price. What they found was a lower price is easy to find, but it's not the price, or the equipment that will make your wedding great, it's the people behind them that make the difference, and that's why they went with us, at our price."*

Or you can try: *"If price is the most important factor when choosing your _____ (insert what you do), then I'm not going to be the right choice. Couples like you don't choose me because they want the lowest price. They choose me because you want (fill in your value proposition – i.e. 'a packed dance floor', or 'guests raving about the food weeks after your wedding', or 'a dress that will make your friends jealous'...)".* Start looking at objections as opportunities and you'll find it much easier to close more sales.

## Negotiating without Lowering your Price

Asking for a lower price is one of the biggest buying signals you can hear. After all, who asks for a discount on something they don't want to buy? People ask for a discount after they've determined that you've met enough of their other needs and wants that they'd like to buy from you. Yes, they're going to ask how much you charge (they can't buy without knowing that), and then some of them will ask for a discount, and I'm fine with that.

### Never get offended when someone asks for a discount

Unless you've never asked for a discount on anything, anywhere – which is highly unlikely - don't be offended when you're asked for a discount. Have you ever asked for a discount, didn't get one and you bought anyway? I'm sure you have. If your customers are only buying when you give them a discount, then you're not selling your services, you're selling the discount, and you have no price integrity. Many of your customers will still buy if you don't give them a discount. If you've done a good job of selling why they should buy from you, and only you, then they have to pay your price. After all, they can't get you and your team anywhere else, at any price.

On the other hand, if they want 'what' you do, but they don't need to get it from you, there's always someone who sells it cheaper. It's very likely that when you were new in business, it was probably you that was the offering the cheaper price. I can't think of anyone I know who started their business as the highest price in their market and category. If your customers can't perceive any difference between buying from you, versus a cheaper competitor, then the lower price will win. Whether tangible, or intangible, you need to make them feel like you're the only one who can fulfill their needs and wants.

## Can you negotiate without lowering you price?

A DJ I met at a networking event told me about how he was handling requests for discounts. Rather than lowering his price, he was offering to divide the total into 3 or 4 payments. I know other wedding pros who are offering even more payments, sometimes dividing the total by the number of months until the wedding. When you do this you're still negotiating, but you're not lowering your price. When someone asks for a discount, and you find a way to give them something, even if it's not a discount, they still feel like you're working with them, as opposed to just saying, no.

## Every dollar you discount is profit you gave away

Remember that it costs you exactly the same to do their wedding or event, unless you take away some products or services. So, every dollar you lower your price, without getting anything of value in return, is profit you gave away. That's why I prefer to give added value, instead of a discount. I once read a study that said, when given the choice between getting 1/3 off, or 1/3 more in added value, more people would choose the added value. That makes sense, especially in our digital currency world. Getting a discount feels good, for the moment. That's true, but you didn't get any more than you were already going to buy. The balance in your bank account is just a little higher than it would have been without the discount. On the other hand, getting added value means you paid the same, but you have something else that you weren't going to pay for – more products, more services, additional time, etc. For example, if a photographer gives a couple a parent album with a value of $300, that costs her $100, the couple gets to give that album to their parents without paying extra for it (both tangible and intangible benefits), and the photographer keeps the integrity of her price. On the other hand, had she discounted her price by $300, she would have lost $300 in profit.

Most people like to get free stuff (although added value isn't really free, because they have to buy something to get it). Celebrities love their swag bags at awards ceremonies, yet they can afford everything in them. I go to lots of trade shows, and I see people seeking out the best swag. I was recently speaking at a destination wedding planners conference in Mexico, and there was so much swag I had to buy a suitcase to get it home. It was my first time to that particular conference, but others told me that one of the reasons they go is all of the good swag. That swag isn't free, it's an added value of attending the conference. They bought their tickets, and the swag is one more reason to attend.

### Finding a "yes"

No one likes to hear "NO," but there are times when you can't give them what they are asking for. Find a way to give them a yes. I read a great quote from Micah Solomon on the Forbes website: "The answer is Yes. Now, what's the question?" What a great sentiment, starting with an attitude of wanting to say yes, every time. If you remember that asking for a discount is a very strong buying signal, then finding a way to give some concession, even a small one, will make them feel that they've been heard. If you're willing to give them a discount, be sure to get something back in return: a larger deposit, higher minimum guest count, remove a product or service, etc. If you lower your price, without getting anything back from them in return, then you're negotiating against yourself.

## Saying no, with a smile

If you don't want to lower your price, then how can you say no without antagonizing them. It's all about how you say no. Don't sound offended. They've just given you a buying signal, this is no time to tick them off. You might say something like this (with a smile): *"Thanks for asking, I know how things can add up quickly for a wedding. After all, we do this all the time. For the particular products/services you want, and for us to have the best team to deliver them for you, the price I gave you is the best we can do to ensure the outcome you want. Would you like me to reserve your date now?"* – Ask for the sale! They've given you a huge buying signal, so ask for the sale. One of the biggest mistakes I see salespeople make is not asking for the sale when they see/hear buying signals. So, the next time someone asks you for a discount, have the confidence to know that if they weren't interested in buying from you, they wouldn't have asked. Don't wait for your customers to volunteer that they want to buy. Help them buy.

# $

## Reduce the distractions during your in-person appointments

Much has been written about the short attention span of Generation Y (the Millennials, who are most your customers of today). It's your job to keep the appointment focused and reduce the distractions. That goes for everything from the physical design and décor of your meeting space, to the background and lighting of your virtual meeting screen. If your business has multiple audiences for weddings, corporate parties, bar/bat mitzvahs, particular ethnic groups, even funerals, it's a good idea to have a way to change the visuals when you meet with them. When a bar mitzvah parent is coming in for a meeting, they should be seeing bar mitzvah art on the walls, bar mitzvah videos playing on your TVs and bar mitzvah images on your printed collateral materials. The same goes for your other audiences. I've seen quite a few wedding pros' offices that use flat screen TVs, instead of printed photos, so they can change the imagery for each audience. So, unless you're a photographer selling large printed and framed photos, you can try this, too. You can also put a nice picture frame around the TV to make it look and feel more like artwork.

### How do they see it?

Sit where they will sit and see what's in their line of sight that might be a distraction. Is there a large window behind you with distracting movement of people, or vehicles? Are there any main-tenance items that need to be addressed, from dusting, to spider webs, to touching up paint and fixing broken ceiling tiles? Look-ing at it from their perspective is one of the things I do when I come for an on-site training. You can't see it the way that they do, because you see it every day, another example of the Curse of Knowledge.

## Say what?

Are there sounds coming from outside or adjacent rooms that might be a distraction? Here's another area where you don't get credit for getting it right, but you lose points for getting it wrong. No one will thank you for reducing the distractions, but they'll notice when it's too noisy, dogs barking, babies crying, and when there are people talking or playing music loudly in the next room. Actually, that wasn't totally correct. You will get thanked in the form of additional business by getting it right.

## Give them your undivided attention

While you're in an appointment, and I know this sounds obvious, but don't take phone calls, check your smartphone, or email. It's rude and it shows them that they're less important than whatever else you're doing. When you're the customer, you don't like that, so, unless someone close to you is about to have a baby, or come out of surgery, silence your devices, and tell you staff (if you have a staff) not to interrupt you unless it relates to this customer. Most of our communication is non-verbal. People believe what they see more than what they hear, and your actions speak volumes. Giving them your undivided attention is key to gaining their trust. I've said this many times, but it's worth mentioning again; people buy from people they know, like and trust.

# S

## SET YOUR PRICE BASED
## UPON VALUE, NOT COST

I was speaking at the Photo Booth Expo, and as you can imagine, there were many, many different types of equipment there. Features varied, as did prices. I was speaking with a couple, who own seven photo booths, and they were considering purchasing a new mirror-booth (a photo booth that looks like a fairytale mirror). There were a couple of different ones that they were considering, and one was a lot more expensive than the other. While the quality of the more expensive one was evident, they were torn on which one to buy.

### Customers buy value, not price

I said to them that, whichever one they decide to buy, they should charge the same price to rent it out. They were confused by my statement, as the more expensive booth was more than double the price to buy. Customers aren't going to have them side-by-side. They're not going to know what you paid or what you didn't buy. They're only going to know what you bring to their wedding or event. And, most importantly, they're not paying you for the equipment, they're paying you for the experience and outcome, which is the fun their guests are going to have at their wedding or event.

This is true for every product and service. While you need to know your costs, you should charge for the outcome and experience you're going to deliver for your clients. Photographers and Videographers have many choices of equipment. Most couples wouldn't be able to tell the difference between photos shot with a Canon, Sony or Nikon camera. DJs and Bands have many choices of equipment. Most customers couldn't tell the difference between the sound of JBL speakers and Bose, or a Gibson guitar versus a Fender. Caterers have infinite choices of kitchen equipment, yet the customer gives no thought to how the food is cooked, just that it wows their guests.

## How do you set your prices?

When you're deciding how much to charge for your products and services, how do you go about it? Do you take your costs and charge a multiple (3 times cost, 5 times cost)? Do you even know what your costs are? Have you taken into consideration your overhead (rent, utilities, insurance, etc.)? Whether it's envelopes, toilet paper or paper clips, the money to pay for them comes from your gross sales.

## If you don't value your time, no one will

Too many wedding and event pros undervalue their time, do you? Do you know how much time it takes to perform your services? Have you included the time it takes to answer their emails, take their phone calls, and meet with them in person (or virtually)? I was sitting with a DJ, who was lamenting to me about another inquiry that asked for his "5-hour package." We started talking about how much time he actually spends on each wedding, from the initial inquiry through any appointments, planning meetings/calls, editing music for each introduction and their first dance, planning their playlist (and do-not-play list) – then the packing up and travel time to their wedding, the wedding itself and then packing up, the time getting home and unpacking. He figured that it was between 35 and 40 hours.

## How much is your 5-hour package?

So, I suggested that the next time someone asks about his 5-hour package, that he reply, something like this: *"Thanks so much for giving me the opportunity to show you how much fun I can make your wedding. I'd love to pack your dance floor, and have your guests saying it was the best wedding they've ever attended. I don't have a 5-hour package, but I'd love to tell you about my 35-hour package – the 5 hours you and your guests will see – and the other 30 hours that I'll be investing, before your wedding, to ensure its success, which you can see from our dozens, and dozens of fantastic reviews."*

Are you charging only for the time you spend at their wedding? Or, are you taking into account all of the other time you're going to invest in them? Too many wedding and event pros set their prices based upon what someone else is charging. How do you know that their prices are correct? You don't. Do you know their costs or profit margin? No. Do you have the same overhead? No. What if their prices are too low (as they often are)? Don't chase them to the bottom.

Over the years, I've challenged many of you to justify your current prices. Can you raise you prices now? Not sure? Ask yourself this: If your prices were 5% higher last year, how many of your customers would have said "No"? If the answer is none, or very few, then your prices are too low. You're undervaluing yourself. When you get to the point where some are saying No, but there would be others who would say Yes to the higher price, then you can still raise your prices. When you get to the point where too many would be saying No, and others would also say No, then you've gone too far.

## Will it work for you?

Early this year I got an email from a wedding pro: *"I put one of your suggestions into action right after the seminar, and increased my servicing fees by $15 per hour, and NOT ONE PERSON objected. Many thanks from my family, because it really was that easy to put an extra $1500 in our family pocket, which means winter holiday in Mexico."* Another wedding pro, a DJ, doubled his prices during one of my presentations, and the next day he sold two weddings at the higher prices! He hadn't raised his prices in years, and had gotten comfortable selling at the lower price, because it was easy. Now, he finds it just as easy to sell at the higher price.

## How much money are you leaving on the table?

Every dollar you raise your prices is extra profit. Conversely, every dollar you discount your prices is profit you're giving away. Take a good, hard look at your pricing structure ask yourself those questions about how many would say No at higher prices, and then see how much more profit you can gain. I look forward to hearing your stories of pricing success!

# To Discount or Not to Discount? That is the question.

A very contentious topic on social forums is discounting. Both sides of the debate dig in, deeply, when this question is posed. To completely understand this subject, the discussion needs to first start with defining discounting versus negotiating. For me, discounting is fine when it has a structure and rules. Everyone who buys the same products/services, for equivalent dates, will pay the same price. The rules are applied equally to everyone. For instance, if you have 3 packages and your higher packages, which contain more services, also have the highest discounts, that's great. If everyone who buys that packages pays the same price, then the rules are being applied equally.

## Explain that to me

On the other hand, negotiating means that two couples, who buy the same products/services, may pay different prices. Each customers' ability to negotiate, or not, will determine their final price. The challenge with negotiating, in today's digitally connected world, is that people can, and will talk about their discount. If you can't easily explain to one customer why they paid more than another customer, for the same products and services - for instance, an in-season date versus an off-season date – then you're negotiating, not discounting.

## Which is right for you?

There's no one answer that's right for every business. Personally, I prefer discounting over negotiating, as it's easier to explain to your employees and your customers. I understand that it may not work for all businesses. In my business, as a speaker, sales trainer and consultant, there is no standard price list. Each event and client involves a different set of circumstances (travel, preparation, residual business, etc.). However, when it comes to my physical products (books, CDs, etc.) discounts make sense. For example, when I have a booth/table at a trade show or event, I'll have my books and sometimes offer an event discount on a package with each of my books. Many times I'll be asked for an even lower price, and I'll thank them, and say that the listed prices are already discounted. Then I'll ask if they want to pay with cash or credit. Asking for a discount is a strong buying signal as people don't ask for a discount on things they don't want to buy. So always ask them for the sale when they ask you for a discount.

## Don't fight the power

One of the keys to having pricing power, is when the customer wants you, specifically you, to do their wedding or event. You're not available anywhere else, at any price. If they don't perceive any difference between you and another company, who has a lower price, the lower price will win. If they can tell the difference, and want you to be their planner, or caterer, or officiant, they have to pay your price.

## Get something of value in return

If you're going to discount or negotiate, try to get something of value in return. If you only lower your price, you're giving away profit. The products and services will cost you the same, but you're getting paid less for them. Whether it's getting a bigger deposit, or being paid in full now, or taking away services, or a higher guaranteed minimum guest count, make them a partner in the negotiation. If you're the only one giving, they'll keep taking. When they want to stop giving, they'll stop asking.

## They'll be back

Many customers will shop around and find a lower price, which isn't hard to do these days. If they do find a lower price, and they still come back to you, they're signaling that they can tell a difference, whether in your products/services, or in the way you've provided a better customer experience, or both. That's an indication that you have pricing power.

They may ask you to match the lower price, but you shouldn't have to in order to get the sale. If they felt the other company would provide just as good services/products and customer experience, at the lower price, they wouldn't have come back to you. The fact that they're coming back shows that they like you and/or trust you more. Always thank them for coming back. After all, if price was the most important factor, you'd be out of the running.

## Price doesn't determine outcome

Sure, sometimes the lower price will win. In these situations a line I often suggest is: *"If price is the most important factor when choosing your (photographer, band, dress, speaker, etc.) then I'm probably not the best choice for your event."* Change the discussion from pricing to outcomes. There are many wedding and event pros who don't charge enough, whether by choice or out of fear. Discounting can be part of a pricing strategy. Negotiating can also be part of a pricing strategy, it's just less structured. There are times when I'll negotiate to get the sale. However, it's the exception, not the rule. If you're receiving something of value in return, or feel it could lead to future business, you might consider coming off your rate.

Rather than lowering your price, I recommend offering them some added value feature (product or service), as it helps to keep integrity in your basic pricing structure. If you're ever thrown in an extra product or service to get the sale, you've negotiated. Some companies do it on every sale. If you give the same, or similar added value services every time, you're really discounting, not negotiating. If the proportionate value of the added services/products changes with every customer, you're negotiating.

## Do I have to offer a discount to get the sale?

Whether you decide to offer a discount, or not, is a personal decision and part of your personal brand. There are many very successful businesses that offer discounts. Sometimes it's due to competitive pressures, and sometimes it's to encourage a higher sale. Packages are a way of using structured discounts to encourage a higher average sale.

## What's the right answer for your business?

I'd have to know a lot more details to answer that. But when discounting becomes the reason that customers book you, instead of them wanting only you to do their wedding or event, you risk diluting your brand. When they're choosing you mostly on price, it's easy for someone else to come along and undercut your price. Whether you choose to discount or negotiate is up to you, just be careful not to get caught up selling the discount, instead of selling the outcomes of choosing your company.

# What a relay race can teach us about marketing

I've often said that wedding pros have more in common than they think when it comes to their marketing. It transcends categories, with photographers, florists, caterers, officiants and dress shops all using the same basic principles when it comes to attracting new business. It also transcends borders, cultures and languages.

I like to use the analogy of a relay race, where a metal baton is passed from one runner to the next. Only instead of runners with batons, you have these steps: Advertising/Marketing/Social Media > your website > email/phone > you. Just as with a relay race, if you need to continue moving the sale forward from stage to stage. Your marketing and sales system is only as strong as its weakest link, where the "baton" is getting dropped the most.

## Follow the bouncing baton

Your prospects find out about you through your advertising, marketing and/or social media. Their next likely step is your website. If they like what they see on your site, they'll email you, use your online availability checker or fill out your contact form. You then have an email conversation with them (phone if you're lucky), and maybe even make the sale at this stage. If you don't yet make the sale, and you have a good conversation, you may get to have a virtual or in-person appointment. If the appointment goes well you get the sale. At each of those points the baton is getting passed. At any, or all, of those points the baton can get dropped.

If your ad is not compelling or well designed, they won't go to your website. If they don't like your social media presence they'll move on. If they do get to your website, but aren't moved to take action, once again, the baton has been dropped. If they do like what they see on your site and contact you, but your email communication skills are weak, you don't get the appointment. If you do get the appointment but your sales skills are lacking, you don't get the sale.

### You don't have to get it right every time

Very few people get it right at every touch-point, which means you're losing potential clients at almost every step. You can never get it right every time, so the goal is to minimize the drop-offs and maximize the "conversion". Conversion is getting someone to take action. Clicking to your website from your storefront on WeddingWire or The Knot is taking action. Clicking from your website to contact you is taking action. Engaging in an email conversation or phone call is taking action. Scheduling an appointment is taking action. And of course, buying is taking action. Those are all positive actions.

Seeing your ad but passing it by and clicking on another ad is also taking action. Visiting your website and leaving without seeing any other pages (it's called bouncing) is also taking action. Emailing you but not agreeing to an appointment is taking action. And of course, coming in for an appointment and not buying is also taking action. These are all negative actions and they're costing you business.

### Accentuate the positive

What you want to do is facilitate as many positive actions as possible, while minimizing the negative actions. How do you do that? Start by plugging the leaks where you're losing prospects:

- Invest in better branding and marketing pieces, from your business cards to brochures, to packaging. Consider hiring a professional designer. You'll usually notice the difference right away and so will your prospects.

- Advertise in the best places, where there are the most prospects. Get the most high-profile placements you can - you can't expect to get the best results with a free or "back-of-the-bus" placement. (You don't want them hiring you because you're free)

- Design better ads, which again may mean hiring a design professional.

- Have a better website experience, probably the most critical link in your marketing chain, since all roads these days lead through your website. This too may require you to hire a professional. The same as with ads, you can't expect the best conversion on your website with a free or cheap site. You want high-quality prospects, you have to "fish" with high-quality "bait".

- Learn how to communicate better via email, likely their first contact method with you.

- Learn better sales skills, or hire a professional salesperson if you don't have the time or skillset.

### Invest in your success

Will some of these things require an investment on your part? Probably, but you want your prospects to make an investment in you to get the highest-quality results, right? Then heed your own advice and invest in yourself and your business so you, too, can get the highest results. Seize every opportunity for education and training. Surround yourself with successful businesses, not just in your own industry, rather successful businesses of all types. What you'll find is that the most successful businesses aren't afraid to make investments in their future and growth.

# What happens when they say 'No'?

In the perfect world of butterflies and rainbows we'd close every sale, for the dollars that we want. But we don't live in a perfect world, do we? There are no trophies for 2nd place when it comes to winning a sale. You either get the sale, or you don't, so what's a wedding or event pro to do? I'd like to give you a little perspective from my many years working in sales and sales management, and more importantly, working with wedding and event pros, like you.

**Here are 5 ways to handle losing a sale:**

1. **Rejection is in the eyes of the beholder** - when you don't get a sale you might feel like you've been rejected, but that's not usually the case. They just liked, trusted, or believed someone else more. Isn't that semantics? I prefer to call it optimism. When it comes to choosing their wedding pro in your category, there can only be one winner. That doesn't make all of the others losers. They may like a few of you enough to hire you, but they have to choose one.

   How many weddings do you do each year? That's how many times they've chosen you and not another wedding pro. Are you the winner? Yes, but you may not have been their only choice. Had you not been available they would have chosen someone else, someone who is very capable, and nice, and likely at a similar price point. So, while this isn't like the 2nd grade, where everyone seems to get a trophy these days for showing up, there's a winner and then there's everyone else.

2. **You often lose the sale before you even had a chance** - Often you lose a sale before you even knew that they were looking for someone in your category. Some couples are looking for you in places where you don't have a presence (Wedding Show, Instagram, Pinterest, The Knot, WeddingWire, etc.). To them you don't exist, but that was your choice. You chose not to be there, or appear on that site or in that wedding show. Or you choose to take the free or cheap listing instead of the more visible, or premium one (Spotlight or Featured). I've often said that if you want others to invest in you, you have to invest in yourself first.

   Other times they make it through to your website but leave without contacting you. They're a legitimate prospect, but you lost them, often without even knowing they had shown interest (going to your website is a very big buying signal). Keeping your site up to date, both technologically and informationally, is critical to plugging this hole.

3. **If they wanted to talk on the phone they would have called** - If you are getting most of your inquiries through email these days (and who isn't?) then you need to make sure you're learning to have better email conversations. If many of your email conversations stop after the first or second reply (ghosting), that's your cue to change the way you communicate. Their first email is likely to ask about price, but that makes sense because they don't know how to shop

for your product or service. You also may not have pricing on your website. According to a WeddingWire survey, 88% of couples are looking for pricing information before they reach out to you. So, if you have no pricing info, at all, on your website, you're encouraging them to ask about price. If your first response is trying to push them to a phone call you're going to lose many of them. Why? If they had wanted to talk on the phone they would have called you.

Customers show us how they want to communicate by the way they contact us. Another reason they don't want to talk on the phone is that they're likely to be at work when they reach out, and they can't (or shouldn't) talk about their wedding during work hours. So if you're trying to force them to adapt to you, and get on a call right away (a high-commitment action), you could be losing out on many opportunities where the leads go cold after your first reply.

4. **Learn from the experience** – Successful entrepreneurs understand that every failure is an opportunity to learn and grow. Take a look at your email exchanges and see if you can identify where the conversation went down, or stopped. If they're going quiet at similar points, or after similar topics, try to adjust your conversations. Also have someone else look at them and see if they can identify any issues. It's often hard to critique your own writing.

5. **Ask why you lost the sale** - Should you ask them why they went with someone else? Sure, the worst that happens is that they don't respond. First be humble and wish them well. Then, if you choose to ask them I think a good question is: *"What did you find with someone else that you didn't*

*find with me (us)?".* That's a lot softer than: *"Why didn't you go with me (us)?".* Asking them: *"What did you find with someone else..."* could give you insight into what their priorities are and why they perceived another company to be a better choice.

Remember that it's not whether you *are* the better choice; it's whether *they* perceive you to be the better choice. It's also OK to be a little upset that you lost the sale. It's not OK to hold onto that anger or frustration. Learn from the experience and do a better job next time. If what you're doing was working a few years ago, and now it's not, it's up to you to learn to adapt. Customers don't adapt to us; we adapt to them. Happy selling.

⌃

# WHEN ARE THERE TOO MANY CHOICES?

I recently attended the Photo Booth Expo, a trade show in Las Vegas. There was a dizzying array of styles of photo booths. There were more traditional booths, reminiscent of the arcades of old. There were very small setups that would fit in a suitcase. There was even someone walking around with her remote controlled, motorized, robot-like equipment. Everywhere you looked there were colors, flashing lights, props, signs and backdrops. Sounds, music and the constant din of voices were coming at you from all angles. It was not the place to be if you wanted some peace and quiet.

## How do you decide?

While I wasn't in the market for a photo booth (I was exhibiting my books and services), I tried to imagine what it would be like if I were shopping for a photobooth, or accessories. How would I decide? Where would I start? So, I spoke to a few of the attendees and asked if it was helpful, or overwhelming, to have so many choices. As with many decisions, there are educated consumers and novices. The more educated consumers came with a mission.

Many had done their research prior to coming to the event. They already had narrowed the choices down to a smaller number, some even looking specifically for one vendor or booth.

For many others, the number of options was debilitating. Each shiny object was its own draw. Each slick sales pitch or marketing promo made promises. With this many choices, how would they decide? Would it be based upon size, or price, or ease of use or maybe the reputation of the manufacturer/distributor? If all other things were equal, what would be the tie-breaker? Or, are there so many choices, that some people will choose not to decide at all?

## The paradox of choice

That's the paradox of choice. When we're the consumer we want to know that we've seen all of the choices; however, in this world of almost infinite choices, how do you decide? How do you narrow down the choices to the best few? And then, how do you narrow those down to the best one? Buyer's remorse happens when you make a decision, and then feel as if you made the wrong decision. It could be that you feel you spent too much, or overpaid (which is a value decision, not a price one). It could be that you think there were other options you didn't yet see. Or maybe that you felt you were pressured into making a decision. Whatever the reason, buyer's remorse is real.

## How does this affect your customers?

In many of your businesses, there are lots of choices. Whether it's which foods for their menu, which dress to choose, which rings to get, or which song for their first dance, choices are all around. When you add up the number of services each couple uses for their wedding (an average of 10 to 12, according to Wedding-Wire), and then the number of choices within each of those services, there are hundreds, or more likely thousands, of choices. It's no wonder that a common reason for not buying that day is that you've given them so much to think about, they need to go home and process it all.

## How can you help them decide?

While it may seem counter-intuitive at first, the best way to help them decide, is to give them fewer choices. I'm not suggesting you should have fewer options - that's a discussion for another time. Rather, you shouldn't present them with as many choices. Your job is to ask them good questions, listen to the answers, and then only present them with the choices that will get them to the outcomes and results that they desire. People buy the outcomes and results. They review the outcomes and results. Therefore, help them decide by finding out what those outcomes and results are, and then show them how the few options - or even one option - that you're presenting to them, will lead them to those outcomes and results.

It's much easier to close the sale when there are only one or two choices in front of them. Reduce the distractions by not presenting options that won't fit their needs. You can present them with options that are above their stated budget, as long as they represent things that will get them the outcomes and results they desire. Don't oversell them - selling them things they don't want/ need and aren't necessary to achieve the desired outcomes. And don't undersell them – let them buy things that will bring them less than the desired outcomes (you don't want to put you name on those products/services, as it's you that's going to get reviewed).

## Be their filter

One of the ways that websites like Amazon.com help us decide is with filters. Depending upon the product, we can filter by manufacturer, shipping options, color, size, and price. We can filter by the average review score. We can sort low to high, or high to low, or newest first or oldest first.  Even choosing how to filter requires decisions, including whether to filter at all, but we need the filters. There are just too many choices. You need to be their filter. You need to help narrow down their choices, so it's easier for them to decide. You need to make it easier to buy, which in turn makes it easier to sell. I don't care how many products, services or packages you have, just don't show them all to any one customer. No one needs to see them all. They can't be right for every customer.

As their filter, you're listening to what they want their wedding or event to be like. You're listening to what they want to feel when they see their photos and video. You're listening to what's most important to them, and then reducing the number of choices that will get them there, and then only present them with those few, filtered choices. It's much easier to close the sale using the choice-close – would you like this one or that one – than it is asking which of 5 choices they'd like to buy.

## What about having 3 packages?

Now, some of you have seen me present on packages, or have read *"Shut Up and Sell More Weddings & Events"* and are asking, *"But Alan, didn't you say that 3 was the right number of packages?"* And if you're one of those people, you'd be correct; I did say and write that. Having 3 packages tends to draw people to the one in the middle, it's called the "Center Stage Effect" by the Journal of Consumer Psychology. But having 3 packages doesn't mean you should be presenting all 3 to every customer. If you determine, through your questioning, that one or more of those packages are not right for a customer/couple, then don't show it to them at

all, it's a distraction. It's the same with showing a wedding couple a marketing piece that talks about your Bar Mitzvah, Prom,
Quinceañera, and Corporate services. They're not relevant to
them, at least not at this time.

Your job is to reduce the distractions, not add to them. Make
it easier for them to decide. Help them avoid "decision-paralysis,"
which is when they are presented with too many choices, so they
decide not to decide at all. As consumers we always decide from
the choices presented to us. So, don't feel that it's your job to show
them everything you do, with countless choices and distractions.
If you've received an inquiry from them, they've already done a lot
of filtering, and you've made it this far. Be the helpful guide and
help them choose more easily.

◀

## Thoughts and Ideas

# When is a Ghost, Not Really a Ghost?

If there's one word that keeps coming up these days it's: 'ghosting.' It's when someone reaches out to you, either through your website, through an online profile (like The Knot or Wedding-Wire), or even through social media, and then when you reply, they seem to disappear. From my experience working with wedding and event pros, like you, there are many reasons why this might be happening. Some of them are easier to explain than others. Some of them are self-inflicted issues (yes, every so often we need to look in the mirror to find the problem).

Here are some possible explanations for why you might be getting ghosted, and what to do about them:

1. **You gave them what they think they need** – if your initial reply has a lot of information, possibly an attachment with pricing or many links, they may think they have everything they need, for now, and there's no need for them to reply. You want to have a conversation with them (verbal or digital). Your price list is not going to close the sale. Your brochure is not going to close the sale. And, if you sent them a PDF, it probably isn't a good user-experience on mobile. Yes, it opens. But most PDFs are made

for full-size pages, some even double pages. Squeeze that down to a phone screen and they're very hard to read.

2. **You didn't ask them a question** – if you've been reading my articles, listening to my presentations or reading my books, you know that I suggest you end each message with one question, the same as you would in-person or on the phone. When you ask a question, you wait for an answer, you don't keep talking. What's been working really well for my clients is to start with low-commitment questions (details about their wedding or event they haven't yet provided) before ramping up to higher-commitment actions... which leads us to:

3. **You asked for a call or meeting in your first reply** – unless they requested a phone call or in-person meeting, asking for one right away is one of the top reasons I see for getting ghosted. If they had wanted to talk on the phone, they would have called you. If they had wanted to meet with you, in-person, they would have asked for that. It doesn't mean they won't have a call or meeting, you just shouldn't push for it without first giving them some information using the communication method they've first used.

4. **You did ask a question, but you buried it** – when you're speaking with someone in-person, or on the phone, you wouldn't ask a question and then keep talking (I hope). So why is it that in emails and other digital communication so many people ask a question and then, they continue writing? Your one, low-commitment question should be the last thing, in its own paragraph so they see it. The only thing after that should be your name and signature (which should also be mobile-friendly). Keep in mind that any

images in your email signature may be converted to attachments when using messenging services (like those on The Knot and WeddingWire). Also, links may turn into plain text.

5. **You sent them away** – take a good look at your replies and look for links to other sites. Do you suggest they look at your social media, YouTube channel, reviews or any other places that aren't on your website? I don't think you should be sending them anywhere. Just have a conversation with them. Actually, you're continuing the conversation they've already started. Which leads us to:

6. **You created a dead-end** – if your message ends with: *"Please feel free to....", "Let me know..."* or *"I look forward to...",* you're creating a dead end. Unless you've arranged for a next step (a call, meeting, or made the sale) there should always be a question or next step. If they want to think about the information you sent, then ask: *"When were you looking to make your final decision on (your service)?"* or *"What other questions can I answer for you now?"*

7. **You gave up too soon** – while it makes perfect sense that if you reply quickly, with a short response and ask a question, they should get back to you, quickly, there are times when it doesn't happen. Yes, you may have followed all of the steps I've outlined here, and in my books and presentations, and you still don't get a reply.

There are a few possible explanations, but it's often that life got in the way. Maybe they just got engaged and sent out inquiries to many different services, not realizing that they need to secure some before others. Maybe they, or someone in their family took ill. Maybe their boss admonished them for planning their wedding or event from work. Many people have told me that they're having success by being persistent. An officiant, who recently attended a Mastermind Day with me, wrote me to say that she had two couples who didn't reply until her 6th message! Both apologized for their late reply saying: *"I just finished my semester and trying to plan a wedding and study for finals was just too much for me!"* and *"I had several messages not showing as new in my inbox!"*, which leads us to:

8. **Your messages aren't making it to their inbox** - maybe your messages just aren't getting through to them. Spam filters, promotion folders (like in Google) and internet gremlins can prevent your messages from making it to their intended recipients. My wife has had the same Yahoo email for years and I've been sending her emails from my Alan@AlanBerg.com address for years. Lately, many of my emails to her have gone to her spam folder, despite the history and despite me being in her favorites and contacts. When I email my accountant, my emails go to his spam folder. I need to use my Gmail address to make it through. You need to try at least two different methods if you haven't heard back after your second attempt.

9. **They've booked someone else** – while you may have done everything right, they still might have reached out to you, and other wedding/event pros, and still booked someone else, yes, without even giving you the courtesy of a reply. Whether it's lack of common courtesy, or they got a great referral from a friend, relative or co-worker and just went with them instead, it's going to happen. I'm not here to defend it, and I certainly can't explain it, so if you've done

your due-diligence (and that's not only one or two tries and then giving up), there comes a time when you have to walk away, knowing you make a valiant effort.

So, there you have it. While this is by no means every possible reason why you're being ghosted, there are many tweaks that you can try to help you get more of them to reply. Remember, if you always do what you've always done, you'll always get what you've always gotten! Try a different approach and see what happens. I look forward to hearing your stories of success.

## Thoughts and Ideas

# SECTION II

# BUSINESS

# A WORLD OF ASPIRATIONAL IMAGES

As a consultant and sales trainer, I get to see a lot of websites and online ad profiles. It still amazes me at how many wedding and event pros are using the wrong images to promote their businesses. For years, I've been saying to use, what I call, Aspirational Images; images that show your prospective clients what the result of doing business with you looks like. When possible, make them so beautiful, and so emotional, that someone viewing it would want to jump into that photo and be a part of the fun, excitement and emotion of that event.

Yet with all of my preaching (which is what it sometimes feels like), there are still countless venues that show pictures of empty banquet rooms; DJs and bands that show equipment, or staff images; florists who show headless brides holding bouquets; and many others who lead with images of themselves. An aspirational image is one that the viewer can take their 'mental eraser' and substitute their face for those in the photo, so they can picture themselves getting that result. We can't get that from looking at your building, or your furniture, or your equipment... or from looking at you.

Don't take my word for it. Here are 3 other resources that say, pretty much, the same thing, in their own way:

1. **Deposit Photos** – a site that I use them to buy images for my blog posts, presentations and articles (please don't

steal images from the internet, you wouldn't want someone stealing your work). As selling images is their business,
they know what works. They posted this on their blog:
*"12 Trends That Will Define Visual Culture Over the Next
12 Months"*. In it, they talk about "authentic images" and
showing "real people in action":

*"When everyone is somewhat of a photographer, the demand
for original, candid and authentic images continues to grow.
Highly visual consumers don't react the same way to polished
photos with posed models; **they want emotions, flaws, the
grit of life, and real people in action**. Relatable photos that
personalize a story and capture a moment (like a Snapchat
story) continue to trend heavily, these visuals have the power
to catch attention and keep the consumer engaged."*

Look for this blog post: "12 Trends That Will
Define Visual Culture Over the Next 12 Months" at
http://bit.ly/12Trends

2. **Pinterest** – don't you wish that Pinterest images came
with price tags? Then the couples would know which of
those beautiful images represent things that would fit into
their budgets. OK, we can all stop dreaming now, and get
back to reality. In a post on their business blog, Pinterest
wrote about using "lifestyle photos" to show your product/
service in use. That means showing people, not just food,
designs and dresses:

*"Your photos should help people understand how your brand would
fit into their lives. **Use real-life settings and models to show how
your product or service can be used**. For example, if you sell
apparel or accessories, feature your products on a model."*

From Pinterest Business: "How to make great Pins" https://
business.pinterest.com/

3. **Facebook** – Even Facebook agrees. When creating ads for Facebook, or really any site, they also suggest that you: *"Show people who are using your product instead of just the products alone.* Remember that your ad may show in someone's News Feed, and it should feel like it belongs there. Your image is competing for people's attention with stories from their friends and family.

    *"Show the benefit that people get from your product, not just a photo of the product.* For example, don't just show a picture of a recipe app to convince people to install it; instead, show the meal they could cook if they use it."

    From "6 Design Tips for Better Facebook Ads" http://bit.ly/6designtips

4. **MailChimp** – I recently read a post on the MailChimp (an email marketing service) blog on social media engagement. It says to use: *"More faces, less copy. People heavy images get more engagement on Instagram, and they can humanize your brand.* https://mailchimp.com/resources/marketing-tips/

So, you can see that this concept is universal. What can you do with this information? Take a look at your website images, your WeddingWire Storefront images, your marketing materials, etc., and see if they represent, not only the outcome that people will get from choosing you, but also that they show real customers getting that result. Real people come in all shapes, colors and sizes, as opposed to models who are setting an unfair bar. Then ask, beg or badger your photographer friends and couples to get images to use. In the end, the effort will be worth it. I look forward to seeing your improved sites and marketing.

## Thoughts and Ideas

# BE THE BIGGEST OR BE THE MOST PROFITABLE?

I love speaking with wedding pros about their businesses, because the business of weddings and events is what my business is all about. Each wedding pro should have your own goals. It's perfectly acceptable to have different goals, at different stages of your business. As a matter of fact, your goals should evolve with your business.

### How do you measure your business?

New businesses are often just trying to survive, while well-established businesses may be trying to stay current and relevant. What are the benchmarks you're using to see how you're doing? Is it the number of weddings and events you do each year? Or is it the total revenue (top-line)? Or maybe it's the bottom line (net profit). Each of you has to decide what's important, and then decide how you're going to achieve that target. Just make sure it's the right target.

### What's in a number?

I was consulting with an entertainment company who told me that he wanted to do 250 weddings the next year. When I asked him why, he said that he felt he would be seen as a major player in his market. I asked why that was important to him and he replied that he felt it would solidify his standing, and how he was viewed by the other wedding pros. When we looked at how he was planning to get there, it was to go after lower-dollar weddings that he wasn't getting now. He was currently more of a boutique business, towards the higher end of his market. As I went through with him how to get to the 250, it occurred to me that he wasn't going to be making much profit on those additional weddings. Once we considered the additional costs: DJs, equipment, insurance, marketing/advertising, admin, etc., most of the money was going to others, not to him. In my words, he was trying to feed his ego, when I'd prefer that he would try to first feed his family.

### Biggest or most profitable?

Another client of mine, a rental company, told me that their goal was to be the biggest rental company in their market. I suggested that a goal of being the most profitable rental company in their market was a better plan. It's often easier to grow your top-line than your bottom line. You can sell more weddings and more services, at or close to your cost, and increase your total sales. Figuring out how to sell more profitable services, or raising your rates and increasing your average sale, is a better plan. You've probably heard the phrase "Work smarter, not harder" and in my opinion, that's a better way to go. When you figure out how to make more profit per wedding, you're on your way to working smarter.

### Which comes first – more weddings or more profit?

If you have the choice to either do more weddings, or increase your average profit per wedding, I'd focus on the latter. When you start making more per wedding, then you can decide if you want to do more events per year, or just make more from doing the same number of events. Many of the pros I meet, and consult with each year, aren't trying to do more weddings. Many have already maxed out the number of events, so the only way to increase their sales, and profit, is to increase their average sale. It's the same for my business. In the early days I was all about increasing my total sales. And while I achieved that, I also realized that I wasn't profiting enough for the amount of sales I was bringing in.

## Diversify, or double-down?

As you look for ways to increase your profits, one possible way is to diversify, and offer new services, or go into new geographic markets. You may see a competitor doing some of these things and decide to follow along. Just make sure that you know why you're doing it, because it's likely you don't know why your competitor is. If you don't know if they're profiting from that expansion, you might be chasing a losing proposition. It's easy to spread yourself too thin, too fast, so think before you follow.

## Is smaller better?

In the lifecycle of many of my clients, they start small, get big (sometimes slowly, sometimes fast) and then, many of them decide to scale back and get smaller again. Maybe it's a venue owner who goes from one, to three, to six venues, and then decides to focus on one or two of the most profitable ones. Or it could be a DJ, photographer or officiant, who goes from being a single-op (just her or him) to multi-op (many employees/contractors, and possibly many services) back to being just her or him and fewer services.

There's no one answer as to which is better. It's about which is better for you, at that time. One thing is for certain, you need to decide how you're measuring your success, right now, and then work to achieve that. Don't follow someone else's idea of success, or you're likely to be like the dog chasing a car. If the dog actually gets to catch the car, then what will it do? If you achieve someone else's idea of success, will you be satisfied? I suggest you choose your own destination, chart your own course, and then enjoy your success when you get there.

˄

# BUILD A STRONG FOUNDATION
# BEFORE YOU EXPAND

Through my many years around the wedding and event business, I've met lots of people who have successfully expanded their businesses, whether it's to other services, and/or other markets. The one common thread is that they already had a successful business before they expanded. I've also run into lots of people who have tried to expand, but failed. Usually they tried too soon, or didn't do the leg work necessary to successfully branch out.

## It's a universal challenge

I was speaking in Mumbai, India, and a make-up artist told me that she wanted to expand to many other countries, and she'd like my advice. I loved her enthusiasm and entrepreneurial spirit. I asked her what contacts she had in those other countries, and she had none. I asked if she had ever visited those other countries, and she had not. I told her that I appreciated her desire to grow, but that she needed to do some research about those markets, how they use make-up services, what the competitive landscape looks like, what the pricing and wedding spending are for services like hers, and lots more things.

## What about you?

Are you thinking of branching out? Countless photographers tell me that they'd love to do destination weddings in exotic places. Why? Probably because they see the photos and posts of other photographers in those places. Who wouldn't want to do that? What you don't see, is what happened leading up to that. How did they get that wedding? What connections do they have that you don't? What networking brought them to that connection? Was that their first destination wedding, or their 20th?

## It all looks great on Instagram and Facebook

The funny thing about Instagram and Facebook posts is that they typically only show the best successes and worst failures. When you see those beautiful destination wedding images on Instagram or Facebook, you don't get the back story. Were there any logistical issues, travel issues or safety concerns? It all looks glamorous on the surface, but you don't hear about the mosquitos, the 16-hour flights, countless hours waiting in airports, hotel issues, or in the case of my recent trip speaking in Mexico, the 10-foot long boa constrictor snake that was outside the venue. Yeah, that's the glamorous part of traveling for work that you don't see, or hear about.

## Becoming the local top dog

Some of you are thinking more local and want to expand to other services in your market, or maybe to an adjacent market. Terrific. The same prep work applies to you as well. Just because a competitor is doing it, doesn't mean it will, or won't work for you. If you're well established in your market, with great connections, that won't automatically translate to another market. You have to build that foundation. The good news is that you're not starting from scratch. You can leverage your reputation and experience.

## But everyone knows me

Name and brand recognition will have to be developed. None of us are national brands with universal name recognition. Coca Cola and Nike have to spend billions of dollars to ensure that their names stay top of mind. With weddings it's even harder, as it's a new crop of engaged couples every year. And, like it or not, there are also new people entering the business side every year. Your contact at that venue may not be there next year. No matter how long you've been in the industry, the hard truth is that everyone doesn't know you. It's no different for my business. When I give a presentation, I often ask the audience how many of them have never seen me speak before. Despite my 20+ years giving presentations, my Certified Speaking Professional® (CSP) designation - I'm one of about 800 in the world - and being a Global Speaking Fellow - as of this writing, one of only 33 in the world, most people in the audience have never heard of me, or seen me present. While it's humbling, it's also exciting to be exposed to a new audience. I can't rest on my laurels and assume that everyone knows me. They don't.

## Go forth and multiply

Don't get discouraged. Just the opposite, I love people who think big. That's a quality in short supply in our industry, with its low barrier to entry. Just remember to do your homework and know what your challenges will be, so you'll be prepared. You'll have to invest in marketing to build that name recognition. You'll have to invest your time in networking to build your contacts. People refer people they know, like and trust. They'll know, like and trust you better if they see you attending, and contributing to local groups and associations. You first have to have the skills that justify you going to another market, service or country. For me it's that investment, plus my network and connections that has led to me speaking in 14 countries, on 5 continents. It doesn't just happen by wishing it. I look forward to seeing your triumphs on social media. You can share your back-story with me when we meet at a networking event.

# Can you Uber-ize your business?

In my frequent travels, I often find myself in need of transportation, either to/from the airport, or to/from a hotel. I started wondering why I'll go on my phone and order an Uber or Lyft car, instead of choosing to get a taxi, when there are often cabs right at the airport or hotel? Often, I could just walk outside find a cab. But, maybe I'll find a line waiting for cabs. Or, maybe a hotel attendant will have to call me a cab. For me, it's the convenience, and certainty, of knowing that I have a ride, and when it will arrive. It's also the convenience of having the charge go right to my credit or debit card, without having to make that physical transaction. It feels more secure to me than swiping my card in countless taxis.

It's also a history of problems I've had with cabs in the past. Things such as dirty cars, long waits and drivers not accepting credit cards, or, as happened to a friend of mine in New Orleans, a driver conveniently telling her he didn't have change of a $20, for her $6.50 ride (he ended up giving her $15 change, short-changing himself in the process). Are Uber and Lyft perfect? Far from it. Many of us who have used them have had our share of less than courteous drivers, cramped cars, and as happened to us at conference in New Orleans, a driver who smelled like alcohol (true story, and Uber refunded my fare for that one).

## How did they do it?

So, what have they done to make Uber and Lyft my preferences for ground transportation, around the world? They disrupted an established player (taxis, limos and car services) by making it easier to do business with them, and by providing information and transparency. Being able to watch the car icon moving along the map doesn't actually get the car there any sooner, but it somehow makes us feel better because we can see the process. In one click we can call or message the driver. Whether you ever use that feature isn't important. The fact that we can is the bigger benefit. Years ago, when toll-free phone numbers were expensive, a large consumer products company put one on their packaging, with wording that encouraged their customers to call, toll-free with any questions. They didn't get that many calls, but the perception of the company in the eyes of consumers, went up noticeably.

## Can you be the disrupter?

Have you thought about how you can disrupt the status quo in your industry category? I remember seeing a videographer's website that had a queue of the weddings that were being edited. It showed each couple exactly where they were in the list, and they could watch their name move up the list – very similar to the car coming towards you in the Uber app. He told me that he used to get numerous emails and calls from couples asking when their video would be ready. Since implementing the online queue, those calls and emails had almost completely gone away. It's benefitted both the customers and the video business.

## I can't do that! (or can you?)

I've met many floral designers who tell me they can't create a proposal on the spot. Instead of doing it while they're meeting with the customer, they need to research and get back to the them, and so they let the customer leave. Not being able to give a price in the appointment, in my opinion, is costing them sales. Customers who are interested are being told to go home and wait for a proposal. Then, you have to get them back in, or chase them down after you've emailed the proposal, only to be ghosted (not getting a reply to your emails and calls). I've also met floral designers who have invested in technology to be able to create a proposal in a manner of minutes, while the customer is still there. Others have told me that they've been in their business long enough that they can make an estimate, on the spot. While they might occasionally be off, sometimes it's in their favor, sometimes in the customer's favor. It averages out over time, but makes them more sales because of the immediacy.

## What was once cutting edge becomes the norm

Toll free numbers were originally only for larger businesses who were willing to invest in them. Then the price came down and we all had them. Credit card processing used to involve expensive technology. Now, anyone with a smart phone can process a credit card, anywhere. Live chat was only for businesses with large staffs. Now, you can live chat on your smart phone from wherever you are. Someone who's out of the office as much as I am used to rely on voice mail. Now, when you call my office phone, my cell phone rings as well. I also use ZipWhip, a service that allows my customers to text my main office land-line. I'm able to see and respond to those texts on my phone, tablet, laptop or desktop.

## Easier to sell is easier to buy

What can you do to make it easier and more convenient to do business with you? How can you reduce the friction, at every step in the process? Having a better website experience, especially the mobile experience, will get you more inquiries. Giving them more choices on how to connect with you will get you more inquiries. Responding better, and faster, will convert more of those inquiries to appointments. Giving them fewer, but better options, will make it easier to sell and easier to buy. You can have dozens of options, just don't show them all to the customer. They can't all be a good fit for their needs and wants. If you hear this often, it's likely your fault for overwhelming them with information: *"You've given us so much to think about, we need to go home and process everything. We'll get back to you."*

## How many choices is too many?

In my consulting with wedding and event businesses, I often help businesses, like yours, scale back your offerings. While it may seem like you're being a better resource by having a multitude of choices, it can often work against you. I see lists of products and services that look like my attic. Stuff goes in, but nothing ever comes out. I once did sales training for a venue that had 12 different chicken dishes on their menu. I asked them why they had so many choices. They said that, over the years, as their customers requested new ones, or their chefs invented new ones, they added them to the list. But, none ever came off the list. I asked how many of the 12 options actually get chosen, and it was 2 or 3. The others were just clouding the decision-making process. Showing all of those options to the customer, before they've reserved their date, was delaying closing the sale. I suggested they remove the 9 or 10 that don't get chosen. Then, make all of the chicken dishes the same price, and just sell them "chicken." Have them choose which kind of chicken *after* they've reserved their date.

I've suggested to many wedding businesses, especially smaller ones who only do one wedding on a day, to only offer one package on their most popular dates. If you get multiple inquiries for those dates, but can only sell one or two couples, why offer your lower package? That is costing you profit. One of my venue clients only offers the "Chef's Tasting Menu" – where the client knows how many appetizer and entrée choices, the main protein, and the chef decides on the actual menu. We've reduced the number of decisions, dramatically. DJ's or Photographers may only offer an "All-Inclusive" package for Saturday nights in high-season. Many wedding venues have "revenue minimums" for certain dates, so why not the rest of you?

### Don't just look at our industry

Pay attention when you're the consumer, and see how what other businesses are doing to make your customer journey easier, can be adapted to your business. Starbucks gets us to pay way more for coffee than McDonalds, yet people line up, every day. I've used Uber in at least 8 countries, all of which have taxis. What are your competitors doing to make it easier to do business with them? Can you disrupt the way business is done in your industry... before someone else does it to you?

## Thoughts and Ideas

## Can your business survive
## without social media?

I attend and speak at a lot of conferences, domestically and internationally, and one of the hottest topics is always social media. Too often I see attendees coming out of these sessions with that deer-in-headlights look. They've just heard someone pontificate about all of the things they need to be doing with social media or their businesses will wither and die. While I agree that social media is an undeniable piece of your marketing puzzle today, it's not the be-all and end-all that some would have us believe.

So, what is social networking and how is it different from social media... or is it? When you attend a local or national trade association meeting, you're doing social networking. You're surrounding yourself with like-minded businesses who are also there to jump-start their success. Social networking has been going on throughout the ages. Connecting with others who have a common interest is a basic human need. Whether it's a trade association, a PTA group or the Girl Scouts, people have and will continue to get together around a common interest. Social media has just added a new dimension by eliminating the need to be physically together. Whether that's a good or bad thing is a debate for another time.

**Let's get real**

I have a good friend who speaks often about how to effectively use social media. While he paints a realistic picture of what you need to do, he's not of the view that your business will die if you choose not to participate, that is, as long as you still do other marketing. I choose not to get into the nitty-gritty details of Facebook, or any other social media, mostly because they change so frequently. I've heard him lamenting about having to check Facebook before each presentation to make sure they haven't changed what he's about to say on stage.

I prefer to take a higher-level view of social media, a more strategic view, similar to how I look at any other marketing. When I give a presentation on social media I start out by focusing on how social media fits into your overall marketing strategy. What's the minimum presence your business should have on a particular platform and how can you use that presence to support your other marketing efforts? I then show real examples of social media pages and posts, and talk about how to improve them. It's very similar to what I do when presenting on websites or collateral materials.

## What's next?

One of the great unknowns is which platform will be the next big thing. There was a time when MySpace was king and that time has passed. I used to connect with old friends from my school days on classmates.com and now I use Facebook. Google+ tried to compete with Facebook, and is now gone. At one time, MySpace probably thought they were unbeatable, too. As of this writing, Instagram is giving Pinterest a run for its money. How long will it last? Your guess is as good as mine. In the short term you want to be where your audience is looking for you. If you don't know where that is... ask them. So, can your business survive without social media? That's entirely up to you to decide.

# CRAIGSLIST IS NOT YOUR COMPETITOR

Just the other day, I heard yet another wedding pro bring up Craigslist (a website where it's free to list products and services for sale), lamenting how easy it is to get into his industry. The thing is, he's at the top end of the price spectrum in his market. Why would he think that people charging a fraction of what he's charging are his competition? It's an easy trap to fall into. Theoretically, anyone who does *what* you do, is a competitor. In the real world, that simply isn't true.

## Is there really a difference?

Technically, Rolls Royce competes with Kia, because their products are both capable of transporting people from point A, to point B. Of course, we know that isn't true. While a Kia buyer might dream about one day owning a Rolls Royce. The opposite isn't so. People buy Rolls Royce cars for reasons beyond basic transportation needs. The same is true when couples are shopping for their DJ, or photographer, or caterer, or dress, or wedding planner. They need *what* you do. Do they need, and want, specifically you to do it?

Marketing expert Seth Godin says (and I'm paraphrasing) that you don't need everyone to want what you do. You only need a small portion of the total market to really understand the specific value you bring. He calls them your 'tribe.' You can't get them all, and you probably don't want them all. Most wedding pros don't want the couple that only has a small amount to spend on their service. Sure, they're entitled to have a fun wedding, with great outcomes. It just may not be the right fit for you to provide those outcomes. Maybe someone else is willing to work for a lot less. You didn't lose that gig to the much cheaper supplier. It was never yours to get.

## What about you?

Are you wasting time, energy and resources worrying about every other company in your market, professional or not? You simply can't control those variables. The barrier to entry for most wedding and event businesses is very low. Many, if not most, wedding service categories don't require a license or certification. Other than those that require an actual physical location (caterer, venue, dress shop...), the monetary investment is very low as well. You don't need the most expensive camera to take great photos. You need a great wedding photographer behind that camera.

Experience can't be bought; it has to be earned. That said, experience is not a guarantee of success. Being in business for 10 years doesn't guarantee that couple a great outcome from you. Have you done 5 weddings each year of those 10 years? Or, have you done 50 weddings each year? Have you updated your technical skills, as well as your business and customer service skills? There are many moving parts when it comes to providing a successful wedding outcome.

## Who is your real competition?

If it's not everyone who does *what* you do, then who are your real competitors? To figure this out, you have to understand how your target market shops for your product/service. What are the things that they value the most? Their priorities drive their budget.

What are they afraid might happen if they make the wrong decision? Fear is a big factor when making a big decision. If they're afraid that you can't, or won't deliver the outcome they want, they'll pay more to someone else for the peace of mind. Those are also the times you scratch your head, wondering why they chose a higher-priced supplier, when you felt you could do everything they wanted.

Maybe, on a technical basis, you could. But the intangibles sent them somewhere else. It may have been something the other company does. Or maybe something they said. Or maybe, how they treated them, from the initial inquiry, to the appointment, to the sale. Most of us have spent more than we could have, because there was something other than price driving the decision. Your competitors aren't every other company. They aren't only the companies that charge less than you.

## Why should they choose you?

We choose to do business with companies, and people, by the way they make us feel about the experience. For weddings, where the consumer is not experienced in shopping for what you do, it gets even harder. They're spending more money than they've ever spent, on things they don't really understand. It's your job to, first, get their attention. Then, get them to make an inquiry. Then, convert that inquiry into a real conversation. Then, move that conversation to an appointment (in-person or virtual), and on to a sale.

So, why should your couples choose you, even if your price is higher? That's the question you need to answer, and then you'll come closer to finding your real competitors. *(hint: the answer is found in your testimonials and reviews!)*

## Thoughts and Ideas

_____

_____

_____

_____

_____

_____

_____

_____

_____

_____

_____

_____

_____

_____

_____

_____

_____

_____

_____

_____

_____

_____

_____

_____

_____

## Do you do weddings or have
## a wedding business?

The good news is that we're in a recession resistant industry. But you already knew that. In most of the categories, there's a very low barrier to entry. That too is good news for many of you, as it allowed you to get in, without much investment. Of course, that also allows many newcomers to get in, every year. Just as many newbies are getting in, many others are dropping out. Hopefully, many are dropping out because they're retiring, after a long, successful career. Unfortunately, many others get out because they can't make it work financially.

Many years ago, I was contacted by someone at Yale University who was doing a research project on the wedding industry. He wanted to find out why so many people get into the wedding industry, when the economics don't seem to make sense. My feeling is that because the barrier to entry is so low, not enough people approach their new venture as a business. Indeed, for many people it starts as a hobby, or sideline. An all too common story is of the hobbyist who gets asked to help out a friend or relative, or themselves at their own wedding, and is then offered money to work for someone else. Sound familiar?

## So, do you do weddings, or do you have a wedding business?

There's nothing wrong with someone getting into our industry that way. It's happened countless times, and it will continue to happen that way. However, nothing about that scenario prepares, or qualifies you to have a wedding business. The skills needed to take pictures, play music, arrange flowers or do calligraphy are not the same ones you need to succeed as a business. Performing a ceremony well, or having the newest, cleanest limousine does not qualify you to have a business. Understanding a balance sheet, profit and loss statement, accounts payables and the various taxes we address is critical to succeeding as a wedding business.

## When did you become a professional?

I like asking wedding pros when they felt they became professionals. Many years ago, one wedding pro told me: *"When I was asked for my insurance certificate!"* That's certainly a wakeup call for many hobbyists. I once referred a friend, who was beginning to DJ events, to my son's fraternity for their annual formal dinner. It was at a very nice Hilton hotel, and of course, their budget was limited. He was willing to work with their budget, that is, until the hotel requested his liability insurance certificate. I suggested that he take the gig, as it would pay for the year of liability insurance, and then he wouldn't have that issue for another year. Instead, he declined the gig! So, instead of doing the gig, maybe breaking even, but having a year of liability insurance, he ended up with no gig, no money and no insurance. That's not a business way of thinking.

So, when do you consider that you became a professional? Was it when you were paid to do a wedding or event? Was is when you did your taxes and had to report the income from your business?

Was it when you were asked for your insurance certificate? I did an online search for the definition of a professional and got this: *"(of a person) engaged in a specified activity as one's main paid occupation rather than as a pastime."* Since I know that many of you either started doing weddings as a sideline (pastime), or maybe are still doing weddings in addition to another job, I don't think this is completely applicable to our industry.

## How much time does it take to do a wedding?

Another great thing about weddings is that they're mostly on Saturday evenings. A WeddingWire Newlywed survey showed that in 2016 half of all US weddings happened on 22 Saturdays. Easy-Weddings, in Australia, told me that 32 Saturdays account for half of all weddings down under. If you have a Monday-Friday job, it's certainly possible to do the Saturday weddings. Of course, there's a lot more to a wedding than what happens that day. There's a lot of preparation and admin that happens before, and in some cases (photo, video) after. Just as people don't see the hours I spend preparing for a speech, whether I've given it before, or not, they don't see the time you invest in making their wedding great. Are you getting paid for that time? Do you charge by the hour for the wedding day, not taking into account the hours you spend before, at and after their event?

## I can do that better!

Many others started their wedding businesses after working for someone else in the industry. Unless it's a capital-intensive category, like a venue or dress shop, that low barrier to entry makes it easy to think you can easily make the leap. I like to remind people ready to make that leap that when it's your business, you pay for everything. The toilet paper doesn't just appear in the bathroom, you have to pay for it. The lights don't go on unless you pay the bill. And the ads don't get run unless you place and pay for them. Doing weddings while you have another paycheck, is a lot easier than doing them as your sole source of support. Some of you have felt that pain. Some of you are still feeling that pain.

## Chin up!

This was not meant to discourage you. Many of you have successful, profitable wedding businesses. Having a successful, profitable wedding business requires investments in time and money. When you're part-time, you can try to do everything on the cheap. Free listings, free apps, etc. I've always felt that if you want others to invest in you, you have to make the investment first. I don't want my customers perceiving that I'm doing everything on the cheap, do you? If you want them to pay your prices, show them that you're leading by example: better graphic design, better website, better messaging and branding, and better continuing education. And then back that up with a better product that gets them better results.

## Which came first?

Notice that I put the better product last on that grouping. You don't get to deliver the better product and results until you make the sale. You don't get to make the sale until you get the inquiry. You don't get the inquiry unless you've done the marketing. How are they going to find you? How are you going to break through the clutter and noise? Those are the things that differentiate hobbyists from businesses.

How are you planning to invest in your wedding business? Have you bought your ticket to a national industry conference? Are you a member of a local association or networking group...

and do you show up to meetings? How are you going to improve your business skills, so you get to perform your technical skills at more weddings? I'll leave you to ponder these and answer them for yourselves.

## Thoughts and Ideas

# It's different, but does that make it wrong?

I've been around the wedding and event industry long enough to see many different business models, from solo-preneurs (we used to call them Mom & Pop shops) to large businesses with many employees and/or locations. None of them is right for everyone. Your business model can, and likely will change throughout the life cycle of your business. I know many DJ's, planners and photographers who started out as just them, grew to many employees and then decided to go back to just them, later in their business' life cycle.

When I started my business of speaking, sales training and consulting, I made a conscious decision not to hire any other speakers, trainers or consultants. I was at a point in my life where I didn't want to have those other responsibilities. That's why my website is AlanBerg.com and not our official company name (Wedding Business Solutions LLC). Had I wanted to have other speakers, consultants or trainers on my staff, I would have chosen a different business identity. That would be different. Not better or worse, just different.

## But that's not the way we do it!

Every so often a new company pops up that has a different business model than yours. I've seen it may times in my 25+ years around this industry. Early in my career selling wedding advertising I had a customer with a wedding photography business. The owner didn't shoot weddings, although she had been a wedding photographer. She just ran the business and had a stable of photographers from which to match with her couples. She had a large, successful business. The solo-preneur photographers in her area hated her. They had all sorts of reasons why, which mostly came down to some variation of: *"That's not the way it's done!"* Maybe not, but did that make it wrong? If her customers were happy with what they were getting, then it was right for them.

I was VP of Sales at The Knot when David's Bridal was started. The small dress shops hated them, complaining of cheaply made dresses, lack of customer service, etc. Their prices were undercutting the local shops and brides were shopping there, despite the lesser quality merchandise and customer service issues. It was certainly different, but did that make it wrong? I had that discussion with many independent dress shops at the time. They threatened to pull their ads if we allowed David's Bridal to advertise. While I felt their pain (their world had been rocked), pulling their ads was only going to accelerate their pain. Cutting off their own lifeline of leads would make their situation worse. The answer was for them to evolve into a world of co-existence with this new business model. Beat them at the things they could do better (quality, the customer experience, etc.) and the customers who valued that would buy from them.

### You can't win them all

It always comes down to the priorities of the customer. If they don't place a high value on quality and the customer experience, and that's all you have to offer them that's different, then the lower price will win, almost every time. If they perceive that buying from you is the same as buying from a lower-priced competitor, then the lower price will win. All new cars will get us from point A to point B, with reliability and safety, yet some people pay more anyway. Similarly, you're looking to attract customers who value the differences between the experience of buying from you versus a competitor. There's always someone with a lower price. As a matter of fact, when you were new in business, it was likely you that was the lower price. I remember having that conversation with my friend David Merrill at an industry conference. David started his event production and design business in his garage and has grown it to an international success. He said that he can't now look down on someone who does the same thing now, just because he's a success. Sure, their business model is different than his, but that doesn't mean it's wrong. His business model has surely evolved over the years.

## Make your own business obsolete, before someone does it for you

I'm always trying to reinvent my business, partly to keep it fresh for you, and partly to keep it interesting for me. Whether it's a new logo, updated website, presentation topic or book, I want to avoid becoming stale or outdated as there's always someone out there who wants a piece of my audience. What are you doing to stay current? What makes your customer want to come back and see what's new, whether it's on your website, in your social media or in your shop/office?

## Thanks for nothing!

I once got a call from a friend who runs a 9-piece band. He had just received his annual Couple's Choice award. While he was happy about it, he thought it had less value because a competitor, who is a large, national company that books DJs and other services, had received theirs as well. If they could get it then, he supposed, it diminished the value of his award. I disagreed with him. His customers were not their customers. Someone who is shopping for a value-priced DJ is not the same person shopping for a 9-piece band, which was many times the price of the DJ. His customers were judging the value of what they received versus what they had paid, and so were the other company's customers.

If the other company was delivering a product, service and experience that satisfied their customers, for the price they paid, then they too deserved their award, and it didn't dilute his award. Just because it was lower-priced didn't mean their customers weren't happy. Nordstrom's exists in a world with WalMart and Mercedes Benz exists in a world with Kia. Some of it has to do with price and some not. You'll likely see Mercedes Benz cars in a WalMart parking lot, and Kia cars in a Nordstrom's parking lot. Just because you can afford to pay more doesn't mean you will. I highly recommend reading/listening to the book: *"The Paradox of Choice,"* by Barry Schwartz, for insight into how people make decisions.

### The latest offender!

I recently had a long-time consulting client complaining to me about a new competitor. Their business model was very different than his, their prices much lower and, in his view, their tactics were unethical. But were they? They are certainly different, but that alone doesn't make them unethical. Are they playing by different rules? Maybe, but that too doesn't make it wrong, just different. I told him that the customers were validating their business model. If there wasn't a market for what they were selling, the competitor would fade away. Just as brides continue to buy from David's

Bridal (despite their recent financial troubles), couples are buying from his new competitor. The competitor is using outside contractors to provide their services, and those contractors are validating the business model by accepting the work. If there were no contractors willing to work for those rates or under those terms, the business model would fail. Different doesn't mean wrong.

## Adapt, don't adopt

I'll mention this in other chapters of this book, but it also has context here, one of the common themes I hear at my National Speakers Association conferences is: *"Adapt, don't Adopt."* Look at what others are doing and then adapt what you see to fit your business... or don't. What works for the other company may, or may not work for you. Just copying what they're doing could be a recipe for failure for you, even if it's wildly successful for them. Want to sell more? Lower your prices to match the competitor. Can you sustain your business that way? Probably not, that's why you charge what you do. Can the competitor? Maybe yes, maybe no. Just as with an iceberg, you don't know the full story, only the part you can see. Your mission is to go about being the best YOU that you can be and find customers that value that uniqueness. There will always be new competitors, but don't chase every shiny new object. You don't want to be like Lemmings, following each other off a cliff.

## Thoughts and Ideas

# SELL IT BEFORE YOU BUY IT

As a speaker and business consultant, I often get asked if it makes sense to add a new service or product to your offerings. Of course, the answer will be different for each business, but we're very fortunate to be in the wedding and event business. Why, you ask? It's because of the lead time between when they book you, versus when the wedding or event will happen. Rather than investing in the new product or service, especially one that's capital-intensive (code for significant financial investment), why not try a different approach?

Let's say you're a venue, photographer or entertainment company, and you want to add photo booths to your offerings. Rather than making the up-front investment in the photo booth, why not start to sell photo booths to your couples whose weddings are happening a year from now. If you have good success, you can buy the booths later, way before those weddings will occur. If you have limited success, you can choose to either buy them, or sub-contract those events out to another vendor who already has them.

## Do the math

It comes down to the return on investment (ROI). Figure out how many sales you need to recoup your investment (and this isn't just about photo booths, this goes for any investment). If, for example, you're thinking about buying up-lights, chair covers or a new wedding arch, how many times do you need to sell them to pay for the cost of buying them? Be sure to include the cost of operating them in your calculation. Let's say you need to sell them ten times to recoup your cost. If, between now and those weddings are happening next year, you're able to sell them at least 10 times, then they're already paid for, before you even get them. If you only sell them 3 times, you have time to figure out why they're not selling, or you can still sub-contract them out to another supplier.

## Does this work for major investments?

You can apply the same logic to other investments, such as getting a larger space. For example, if you're a floral designer or caterer, and you're thinking you might need a larger prep space or commercial kitchen, first sell those additional weddings and events, then before next year when those events happen, get the larger space. If you'll only need larger space for a few events, maybe you can sublet space, as needed, only for those times (so you're not paying that overhead all the time). With something like real estate, give yourself enough lead time, as it's often harder to find and get the space permitted and inspected, than to buy the new equipment.

## But all the cool kids have it

Too many wedding pros have things sitting on their shelves collecting dust, instead of creating revenue. I know how you get caught up in the moment at the trade shows. It's exciting to get the new, shiny object... that is, until you find out that no one wants it for their event. It's also tempting to look at what others are doing, and jump in, head-first, before doing a reality-check.

I once had a DJ call me and ask if I thought he should buy flat screen TVs. I asked why he was considering it. He said that all of his competitors had them. I said, OK, but why are YOU considering them? He reiterated that his competitors had them. I asked if his customers were asking for them. He said, no. Then I asked if he suddenly needed two for this weekend, could he get them. He said, yes. So, I told him not to buy them... yet. I suggested that he start offering them for events at least 6 months out. Then, if his customers are buying them he can consider making the investment. If he doesn't do well selling them, he can rent them for the events where he needs them.

## Will this work for everyone?

This thought process can be applied to many investments, but the more lead-time you have, the easier it is to implement. If your time from sale to event is only days, weeks, or a few months, it might be harder to get the equipment, become proficient with it and use it effectively for your clients. If you can rent the equipment, as needed, and let the maintenance be someone else's problem, that too might be viable option. You could also end up with the latest technology, every time you need it, instead of aging technology that you own. For instance, if you occasionally need a larger truck, you can rent one, instead of having one that's too large for your everyday needs.

Remember that before offering a new product or service, you need to be able to do deliver a successful outcome. If you were the customer, you wouldn't want someone learning it on the day of your event, and neither do they.

## Thoughts and Ideas

# There's Always a Cost

I was once conducting a private group mastermind and the discussion turned to investments versus expenses. I remember reading that business people, including most CEO's, almost always look first at the cost of an opportunity, before asking about the potential return. I guess it's just human nature that when presented with an opportunity you want to know how much it's going to cost you. Then it dawned on me... there's always a cost, but it's not always money.

**What's the cost?**

Whether it's for your business, your family, or in a personal relationship, there's always a cost of taking, or not taking action. Your cost may be:

- Time
- Money
- Emotional capital
- Or some combination of the above

Deciding to start a business, or change jobs, costs you all of the above. Investing your time in a business or a new job of course takes money, but it also takes time, which affects your personal relationships. How much emotional capital are you willing to lose (time not spent with your family, your loved ones and friends) because of the time you're spending on your new path? That's as important of a decision as how much money you want to invest in your business.

## The cost of inaction

Conversely, what's the toll on your family if you don't take that new job, or start that business? I'm in this industry because I was miserable in a good paying job. I had a company car and good benefits, but I loathed going to work every day. My wife was expecting our second child, our son was 3, and I was never home. I like to joke that I only worked ½ a day... 12 hours from 9am to 9pm. Many of you can relate to that. So, when a friend called and asked if I would come and sell wedding advertising for the magazine he just bought, commission only, no salary, no base pay, no draw against commissions, no guarantees—and I'd needed to buy a car—I jumped at it.

Looking back on it, the costs were huge. I gave up the security of the good pay. I gave up not having to pay for a car. I gave up the good benefits which protected me and my family. I also gave up the stress of going to a job I hated. While I didn't give up working long hours, I had more control over those hours. On paper it seemed like a risky path. While living it, I knew I was making the right decision.

## Avoiding hypocrisy

I've never met a wedding or event pro who didn't want to get paid well for the services you provide to your clients. I'm more likely to hear complaining about how you can't charge more (which is a discussion in another chapter). Then why is it when you're looking for a product or service, or when you're presented with an opportunity, you look for the cheap solution? Free advertising. Do you make your own website? Design your own marketing materials? We all want people to invest in us, so we have to invest first. If you were a building a new venue you wouldn't expect people to reserve it for their weddings, unless they see that you're investing in it first. You wouldn't say: *"If you give us a deposit we'll build the facility."* Even if it was under construction they can see that you're already investing. That's why new home builders build model homes, furnish them beautifully and hire professional graphic designers and marketers for their sales materials. They invest first, then you invest.

I'm not immune to wanting to save a dollar here and there, but not at the cost of quality or how it represents my brand. I had tried a few online printing companies for my marketing materials, but I experienced inconsistent colors and quality. Now, almost everything I print goes to one or two printing companies, and I don't look at whether I can save elsewhere. These have quick turnaround, consistent quality and responsive people. My time is valuable, and any of it that I spend dealing with a supplier is costing me both time, and money.

## Why spend more?

There are times when you're presented with an opportunity with multiple options, at multiple price points (kind of sounds like what you present to your clients). Do you always look at the lowest priced option first? Or do you look for which will get you the highest return, the best outcome, and then look at price? Having been behind the scenes at sites like WeddingWire, The Knot, weddingsonline (Ireland, Dubai & India), Easy Weddings (Australia) and Guides For Brides (UK), I know that the people spending the most, are usually the ones getting the best return. Does it cost them more for their placement? Yes. Is the return bringing them more than the additional cost? In almost every case I've seen, the answer is a resounding Yes.

## When should you decide to spend more?

What do you tell your clients? You tell them that if they want the outcomes that they've expressed to you, they often have to spend more. Then look in the mirror, and tell yourself the same thing. If you want a better return, be willing to make the investment first. When I left The Knot, after 11 years there, I said to my wife: *"If I can't look in the mirror and tell that guy how to start, and run a successful business, and be willing to take the actions, and make the investments necessary to do that, then no one should hire me to help them with their businesses."*

Lead by example. Think about some of the things that clients do to you that frustrate you. Are you doing those same things when you're the customer? There's always a cost. What do you get if you choose the cheaper, or free option? What do you get if your just choose not to decide? The opportunity-cost of inaction is often greater.

# Upgrade to the Platinum Rule

Y ou're probably familiar with 'The Golden Rule': *"Do unto others as you would have them do unto you."* While that sounds like a great plan for life there's something inherently flawed with the concept. We're not all the same, we don't like the same things and we don't necessarily like to be treated the same way. It's sometimes cultural, regional or situational. For instance, I grew up in New York City where people can be a little more direct than in other areas. It's not better or worse, just different than what someone may have experienced growing up in Kansas or Mississippi.

When someone is a little more direct with me, I usually don't take offense, while someone who is not used to that might feel a sting. Our words and actions are received differently by different people in different situations. Someone barking orders at you would be perceived differently in a restaurant than in a burning building or at boot camp. Our tone and body language will also affect how we're perceived by others.

## The Platinum Rule

So, if treating others the way would want to be treated is imperfect, what should you do? Great question. Dr. Tony Alessandra wrote The Platinum Rule: *"Treat others the way they want to be treated."* Of course, that makes perfect sense. They want to be treated a certain way and that's what we should do. That may, or may not be the way you want to be treated. This applies in our personal lives as well as our businesses.

## Mirroring and reciprocating

A basic rule of sales, and interpersonal connections is to mirror the other person. This applies in person and in your other inter-actions (phone, email, text, messaging, etc.). A WeddingWire study showed that nearly half of couples surveyed get frustrated when you don't reciprocate their chosen communication method. When they email or message you and you want to have a call or meeting, right away, that's causing friction. You're not doing unto others the way they want you to. You're doing unto others the way you want them to do to you. The more friction you add to the sales process, the more they'll look to someone else, no matter how good your work or reputation.

This is not a generational thing this is a people thing. I recently had a situation (that prompted this article) that highlights this principle. My wife and I are shopping for a particular insurance product. So, I went online and filled out a contact form (sound familiar to our industry). The next day I got a phone call from a sales agent. Would I have preferred an email? Yes, but I didn't mind the call as I had some time when she called. That said, her first request was to set up an in-home meeting with my wife and I. I explained to her that with my travel schedule that would be very difficult, and I preferred that we communicate via phone and email. Again, she pushed for the in-home meeting.

## Who's the customer here?

I politely told her that I was already very familiar with this type of insurance and that I could give her whatever information she needed, right now (since we were already talking) and then she could email me some quotes and options. I could feel the frustration on her end as she again resisted. So, I politely asked her: *"Is there someone else I can speak with?"* She was taken aback by my request. I asked that if she couldn't do business the way that was convenient for me, was there someone else who would/could? She relented, a little, and said she would work up some quotes and email them to me. While I got what I was looking for, my feelings for working with her were already diminished. When I emailed her for another quote option, her reply began with: *"This is why I sit with all my clients to go over all details to explain the variances and find what makes the most sense."* Can you feel her attitude here, or is it just me? Just give me the information I requested!

## We all have choices

So, what did I do? I reached out to another company to get a comparison quote. I remembered that an industry friend also worked in insurance. I reached out and he connected me with someone with whom I also had a call, and then all of our following communications were via email. He never pushed for the in-home meeting. I never felt the friction in the process that I did with the other agent. And when I asked, via email, for another quote option, his response was fast and friendly:

> *"Hi Alan,*
>
> *Thanks for taking the time to speak with us today. Here are the quotes we discussed...*
>
> *Dominic"*

When I asked him for the other option, his reply was:

*"Certainly Alan, see attached. We will be in the office tomorrow if you'd like to schedule a call.*

*Thanks!"*

Which agent do you think is getting my business? Dominic, of course.

## Is this why they're ghosting you?

Are you unknowingly adding friction to the process? Do you know how your prospects are perceiving your tone or attitude? If you're getting ghosted on many of your replies, one possible reason is that you're not using the Platinum Rule. If your first reply to an inquiry asks for a call or meeting, you're adding friction. Sure, it may work sometimes, but you may be chasing away as much business as you're getting, or more. I mentioned in another chapter that people do business with people they know, like and trust. If you mirror their tone (formality), their energy (excitement level) and the way they communicate, they'll feel more comfortable doing business with you. If you don't, you'll add friction, and the more friction you add, the more likely the sales process will stall, or stop. Start applying the Platinum Rule, and you'll reduce the friction and make more sales!

## Volume versus profit

In my conversations with wedding pros, around the world, one topic that often arises is how many weddings/events your business should do each year. There's certainly no one answer that's right for every business. So many factors will affect both your ability and desire to do more weddings/events. If you're just starting out, and maybe still holding down a full-time job, outside the industry, there's certainly a limit to how many weddings you can do effectively. On the other hand, if you're a well-established wedding pro, maybe even looking towards retirement, you too may be looking to do a smaller number of weddings/events.

### Growth strategy

What about businesses who are on the growth curve? There are different ways to grow your business. One is to grow the volume and another is to grow your average sale. Given the choice between those two, I would choose to grow your average sale first, so you earn more from each wedding/event. Then, if you choose to increase your volume, over time you'll earn exponentially more. Before you decide to do more weddings/events, think about why you want to do more. If it's to impress your industry friends, or as one wedding pro told me, to be seen as a major player in his market/category, make sure you're also increasing profit. I've often said in my consulting that I don't want to feed your ego, if we're not also feeding your family.

## Keep your eye on the profit

Regardless of which way you go, keep an eye on your profitability. Growing your top line is easy if you're giving it away. Growing your bottom line is the better long-term strategy. Take a close look at your costs, the time it takes you to complete an event and your pricing. Costs are relatively easy to find. You should know what the products, ingredients and raw materials cost for each event. Be sure to include everything you use, whether it comes off your warehouse shelf, or your kitchen shelf.

Time is something that seems to be harder for wedding pros to quantify. You invest time with each wedding/event from the moment you get an inquiry. How much time do you invest replying to their emails, calls and in meetings? It's not just the time on the day of their wedding, it's also all of the time before and after. For some, particularly videographers, there's more time spent after the wedding than before or during. How much are you getting paid for your time? Would you take a job that paid that hourly wage?

## The 40-hour wedding

While I was having dinner with Ron Ruth, a wedding DJ friend, he received a new inquiry that asked: *"How much do you charge for a 5-hour wedding?"* We can't blame the couple for the question, it's the wedding pros who are selling their services that way that create that environment. If wedding pros only value the time they spend at the actual event, and not the time they invest before, and after, then we can't expect couples to value that other time, either. When I asked my friend how much time he actually invests in each wedding, he said it was somewhere between 30 and 40 hours. Given that he does a 'Grand Entrance', cuts and edits different music for bridal party introductions, displays photos, does a lighting plan and more, that's a reasonable estimate. If he were to price his services, by the hour, for only 5 hours, his effective hourly rate is actually 1/6 of that. I suggested that he reply by saying: *"Thanks for reaching out. I'd love to make your wedding amazing, pack your dance floor, and have your friends and family saying it was the best they've ever experienced. I don't have a 5-hour package, but I'd love to tell you about the 35 hours that I'm going to invest in making your wedding great."* – and then ask one low-commitment question to keep the conversation going.

## What's the value?

So, how should you price your product and services? Given that many wedding businesses are service businesses (and yes, we can certainly say that ALL are service businesses, even those with tangible products), it's really about your time, your creativity, designs and ideas. How do you put a price on those? Do you price based upon what others charge? Do you take your expenses and then mark them up? Or, do you set your prices based upon the value that you are bringing to both your couples, and to you and your family. You see, you set the price, your customers determine the value. Regardless of the price you set, if you need to discount to get the sale, then the actual value is the price the customer paid, not the original price.

## Giving away profit

Remember that every dollar you discount is profit you gave away. Conversely, every dollar you raise your prices is additional profit you earn... provided the customers are paying the new, higher price. So, the next time you are asked for a discount, ask yourself how much of your profit you want to give away. Your customers are entitled to ask for a discount. When we're the customer, we have that right as well. You, the business, have a right to say yes, or no. Just ensure that you're profiting, regardless of your discounting policy. And, if you'd like to see how you can profit, from day 1 in your business, I recommend reading: *"Profit First"* by Mike Michalowicz. It'll change the way you view profit, for the better.

⌃

# What's a Good ROI?

If you're like many wedding and event pros, it was your creativity that brought you into the industry, not necessarily your business acumen. To have a successful business, you need both. There are lots of hobbyists who are very creative. Once you decide to sell your products or services, you need to develop your business skills and an understanding of the many ways to measure your success.

### How do you measure your business success?

Some wedding pros like to brag about the number of weddings they do. Others will talk about their gross sales. Of course, any good financial advisor or consultant will tell you that it's not what you make, it's what you keep. In the early years of your business, you should be returning back much of your profits (if you have any) into growing your business. I've often heard that a growing business should be investing 10%-15% of their anticipated sales, into their marketing and advertising. Not 10%-15% of their actual sales; the higher sales number that they're trying to achieve. Then, once you've gotten there, you can lower that percentage to maintain your sales.

### Don't shut off the engines

It's like the analogy of how a pilot needs to have the throttle on full to get the plane off the ground and to get to cruising altitude. Once at cruising altitude, a pilot doesn't turn off the engines, they back off enough to keep them up there. If they need to climb - maybe to avoid bad weather - they increase the throttle. Similarly, if you want to increase your sales, or you expand into a different market, or a new service/product, you need to increase your marketing/advertising budget, again.

## What's a good ROI?

How do know if you're getting a good ROI (Return On your Investment)? The short answer is that you have to measure it. In the real world, that's sometimes easier said than done. While it's easy to see some online metrics, much of what happens either isn't tracked or you can't connect the dots easily. For instance, when someone gets to your website, and sends you an inquiry, that's great, but where did that lead really come from. I've often said that we don't get any business 'from' our websites. We get business 'through' our websites. They had to come 'from' somewhere to get to our sites. And, what if they were at three or four other sites before they got to your site? Now, where did that business really come from?

## What are you tracking?

Too many wedding and event pros are asking the wrong tracking questions - at the wrong time. For instance, if you're waiting for a phone, or face-to-face meeting, to ask: *"How did you hear about us?"*, that's both the wrong question and the wrong time. You're too far removed from all of those online clicks. A better question, right on your website contact form, is: *"How did you find our website today?"* It's the closest you'll be to that last click. If you have analytics for your website, it's not likely to be sophisticated enough to show you the path for that specific customer, before they got to your site. Marketing Guru, Seth Godin, wrote: *"The last click someone clicks before they buy something isn't the moment they made up their mind."* Before they got to your site, they were already thinking about your product, or service. You just can't see all of those other steps.

## The basics of ROI

The difference between an investment and an expense, is that an investment may return you more than you invested. While an expense gets you only what you paid for (gas, your vehicle, your computer, etc.), to calculate your ROI, you need two numbers: the amount you spent on that investment and the amount you got in return. You can never say whether something is expensive, or inexpensive, based solely on the price. While one professional camera may cost twice as much as another, it may have features that will help a particular photographer make more sales. If those additional sales justify the extra investment, then it's not expensive. However, the same camera to a different photographer - with no way to monetize that feature - may be considered expensive.

## All ROI are not created equal

Of course, not all investments return the same ROI, nor should they. There's usually no connection between different investments, so comparing their ROI is an imperfect exercise, at best. What we need to do is measure each investment's ROI, on its own merit. From a business and financial perspective, does this particular investment make sense? The opportunity cost of choosing one investment over another is the potential profit of the investment you didn't make - if it could be higher than one you're making now.

But, that too, is an imperfect analytic. In the real world, it gets more complicated. For instance, let's say you were thinking of doing a particular wedding show, so you decide to move some of your advertising dollars, from something else, to that show. While that seems like a sound decision, in the real world, any couples who would have found you on the ad you dropped, won't find you at the show, or even on a different website. The couples who choose to attend a particular wedding show, or frequent a particular website, won't go looking for you elsewhere if they don't see you. They'll choose from the vendors they see where they are (on that site, or at the show, etc..). If you have a positive ROI from the ad you're thinking of dropping (you're making more in profit, than you're spending), then you're going backwards by dropping it. The new investment needs to bring you at least the same profit, or you're going backwards. Of course, you won't know – until, or unless you try it.

## Don't bet the rent money

What I suggest to my clients, businesses just like yours, is to find additional money with which to try the new opportunity. Once you prove that it works, and brings you in a better profit, you can decide if you should drop something else. However, if they're both bringing in a good profit, even if those profit margins are very different, don't shoot yourself in the foot (or rather, the bottom line). The only time I'd drop the lower-performing investment, is when the new one is filling your calendar; if it's not, then you need both.

## No one likes a rate increase

Every so often, I'll have someone complain to me about a rate increase they got from a marketing or advertising platform. Sure, none of us likes to get an increase, but I often present on getting you to raise your rates, charge what you're worth, and account for your increasing costs. So, it's kind of hypocritical to raise our rates and complain when another business does it to us. What I always suggest, is to take the emotion out, and look at it rationally. Don't look at what the rate was, look at what the new rate is, and does the ROI make sense at the new rate.

## Final thoughts

One of the most important metrics is profitability. I don't care how many weddings or events you do. I'm not impressed if you double the number of events you do, but your bottom line doesn't increase. My goal is to help you be happier and more profitable. I have several industry clients who've cut back on their number of events, so they can concentrate on more profitable business. If your ROI from two different ads, or opportunities, is the same, it's a coincidence. Before you start jumping from one opportunity to another, take a look at your ROI for each one, over time, and not in comparison to the others, rather on its own merits.

## Thoughts and Ideas

# WHO'S IN YOUR NETWORK?

I once presented at a local wedding association meeting who, opened the workshop to non-members, as a gesture to help educate the industry (and I'm sure it wouldn't hurt to try to drum up a few new members). As is the case at all meetings like this, many of the people who attended already knew each other. Many already get together outside the meetings, either socially or to network.

## Is that a clique, or a network?

There's a fine line between a clique and a network, but it's often hard to see the difference from the outside. For me, the difference is whether the group is open to new members. When I say group, I don't necessarily mean a formal association. At workshops and conferences, wedding and event pros tend to cluster in groups. I'm sure a psychologist would tell us that this is natural, human behavior. Are those groups cliques? They can often feel impenetrable, because the body language of the group feels exclusive, as opposed to inclusive. Outsiders often don't try to join the group, assuming, in advance, that they're not welcome. Sometimes that's the case, sometimes it's not.

## Who's in your five?

Do you remember the cell phone ads that used the line: *"Who's in your five?"* For us, your 'five' is your inner-circle (which can certainly be more than five people). Who are the industry connections with whom you socialize? It's been said that we do business with people we know, like and trust (credit to Bob Burg, no relation). When a couple asks for a referral to another service, or when you're booked and want to refer a colleague, why do you refer those particular people or businesses? Is it just because they're the best at what they do? Or, is it because they're good at what they do, and you saw them recently, either at a wedding, or at a networking event, or over coffee last Tuesday?

## How can you expand your network?

First, remember that you weren't always on the inside. Too often I see wedding pros complaining about the new company in their market, whether they're a lower-price, or a direct competitor. Weren't we all the new guy (or gal) at one time? Weren't our prices lower than many, if not most competitors, when we were new to the industry? For many of us, the answer to those questions is yes. Rather than shun these newbies, why not welcome them into the fold? Wouldn't it have been nice if you had been welcomed that way when you were new? Or, maybe you were we.

## A rising tide raises all ships

Welcoming the new businesses, and helping them do things the right way, helps everyone. We all know that it only takes one person, in your market and category, to provide bad customer service, or to take advantage of a customer, to make us all look bad. I would rather compete with someone who's doing things well, and is honest and well-respected. It help keep me sharp, and on top of my game.

## You can teach an old dog...

Another reason to widen your network with newcomers is that they often have new ideas that can help you. Those of us who've been at our craft for a while can sometimes get set in our ways. Have you ever been caught off-guard by a newcomer who's taking market share with their new approach? Baby-boomers and Gen Xers can learn from millennials and vice versa. You may like your way, but it's not the only way. Regardless of age, none of us can learn anything new if we're not open to the possibilities. So, the next time you find yourself in a group, and you see someone you don't know, try introducing yourself and inviting them in. You may make a great business connection, or even a new friend. Who's in your five?

## Thoughts and Ideas

## You get what you measure

I received a call from a client's sales manager asking me how many calls I expected my sales reps to make. I told him that throughout my sales career in this industry, beginning when I was an independent ad sales rep (commission only), then a publisher (with 3 sales reps), to a Regional Sales Director (16 reps) and then VP of Sales (over 50 reps), I never measured phone call volume. He seemed surprised, as that's been one of the metrics he'd been judged by as a sales rep most of his career, so he was using that as a benchmark for his team.

I explained that, at least to me, measuring call volume was a distraction, as call volume was not what I was trying to achieve. More sales was the goal, so that's what I measured. I never asked my sales reps for call reports, or used systems to measure their call volume... that is, unless they weren't making their sales numbers. If the production wasn't there, then I wanted to know what they were doing. Interestingly, my top performing reps often made the fewest calls. They just had more productive calls. My lower-performing reps were often making lots of calls, but they weren't going anywhere.

### What's your benchmark?

What are you measuring in your business, or life? Is it in alignment with what you want to achieve? Sales volume is certainly a good measurement, but profitability is a better one. It's easy to increase the number sales you make, just lower your prices until everyone says Yes! I don't know about you, but that's not what I'm looking to achieve. What about sales dollars? That's a better benchmark, but as with sales volume, it is an incomplete measurement.

You may want to spend more time with your family. But, if you have your eyes glued to your phone while you're with them, what did you really accomplish? The key to accomplishing your goals is to set better ones. Make them lofty, but realistic. Don't set yourself up for failure, set yourself up for success. A wall just a foot above the ground is an easy bar to walk over. One twenty feet high is nearly impossible one to surpass. Definitely reach higher, but also have a realistic plan to get there.

## Measuring conversion

I often get asked about conversion percentages, in other words how many of the leads you receive should you convert to a sale. Of course, there is no one right answer, because there isn't enough information for me to compare apples to apples. If one wedding pro's website has clear pricing information, while a competitor has none, the second business may end up fielding many inquiries who can't afford them, artificially increasing their inquiry numbers, and decreasing their conversion percentage. If you want to measure conversion, you need to be looking at how many visitors come to your storefront or website and then take a next step (make an inquiry, or click through to your site from your storefront and then make an inquiry). That's going to be really hard to track, unless you have very good website tracking software... and you know how to properly read it.

That said, you can track inquiries to conversations, and conversations to either appointments (or sales), and appointments to sales. You need to keep good records. The first rule of computers that I learned was the acronym GIGO – Garbage In, Garbage out. If someone makes an inquiry, but you're already booked on that date, and they can't/won't change their date, that was still a good inquiry. Unless you have an availability calendar, so they can check their date before reaching out, those are valid inquiries. Quick side-note – as some couples change their wedding date, for most of you, I'd suggest it's better to get the inquiry and find out that you're already booked, than not get the inquiry at all. We know from a WeddingWire survey that nearly 90% of couples are looking for price before they reach out to you. So, displaying some kind of pricing guidelines is beneficial to getting more and better inquiries. And yes, I know that many of you don't want to display pricing, but when you're the customer, aren't you looking for price?

**Inquiries, Conversations or Sales, Oh My!**

So, what should you measure? Start with the easiest things to measure, which would be inquiries (whether through your website, your storefront, direct emails, social messaging, etc.). Then measure how many of those you get to have meaningful conversations with, through the method by which they've reached out to you (which is how you should initially be responding). Then see how many of those conversations become sales directly, or lead to a phone call, Skype/web call, or in-person meeting. And of course, track how many of those meetings turn into sales.

You'll want to track the conversion from each source separately to see where your best leads are coming 'through'. Notice I didn't say where they're coming 'from.' The reason is that you don't get business 'from' your website, you get business 'through' it. They had to come 'from' somewhere to get to your website.

Your couples, just as when you're the customer, make many stops along the way to get to you. You'll probably never know all of them, just the last one or two, and if they also were referred to you by someone they know, you may get that as well. It's an inexact science, at best.

## What's the trend?

Reporting like this is most helpful by watching trends, rather than discrete numbers. You need to see how these conversions are trending over time so you can have visibility to improvements and degradations. If you change something on your advertising store-front (like adding pricing, or updating photos and videos, or getting a higher placement), did it make an impact on your inquiries (and click-throughs)? If you updated your website, or better yet, built a new one, did it affect your inquiries? However, don't forget that you get what you measure. So, keep an eye on your sales and profitability numbers as that's really what you want. Higher sales volume without higher profit is a poor outcome. It's nice to say you did more events, but not if it's not flowing to the bottom line. As I've said before, I want to feed your family, not your ego!

# SECTION III

# INSPIRATION

# Are you a thought leader or a follower? Your success depends upon the answer.

I was attending and speaking at a Wedding conference in Cancun and I had the pleasure of meeting and hearing Michael Nolte (noltesbridal.com). He spoke about the difference between Brains and Bluster (my word, not his). Those people that come up with new ideas (brains) versus those that purport to be industry experts, when all they're really doing is talking about what others are doing in the industry (bluster). The bluster often gets attention, while the brains are busy creating new ideas and getting it done.

That got me thinking about each of you. Are you a thought-leader or a follower? Put another way, are you the shepherd or a sheep? It's OK to get ideas and inspiration from what you see others are doing. That's natural. What you want to do is make it your own. As I've said before, the National Speakers Association has a saying: *"Adapt, don't Adopt"*. That means you can take inspiration from something new and unique that someone else is doing, just find a way to make it your own. If you hear me speak and tell a story, don't use my story in your speech. Rather, find a story of your own that brings your audience to the same meaning or conclusion.

## Stealing or Research?

Wilson Mizner said: *"To steal ideas from one person is plagiarism, to steal ideas from many is research."* I agree with the premise. Taking inspiration from many different people and then coming up with your own version of that "stew" is not only acceptable, it's inevitable. I even use these words on my "About Me" page on my website: *"We're all a product of our experience and mine has been quite varied"*.

It's impossible to forget all of the things you've seen others do when creating your products and performing your services. Composers can't suddenly forget every song they've ever heard when writing a new song. Floral designers can't forget every centerpiece they've ever seen others do when creating a new design. Chefs can't erase the memory of everything they've seen other chefs make when creating a new dish.

The idea is not to forget the past, it's to use what we've seen and learned and put our own spin on it. Come up with your own "signature style," "signature dish" or "signature story". Your experience is unique. No one else in the world has ever had the same experiences as you. Sure, you've usually shared each experience with one or more people. But those other people haven't been there for every experience your entire life. Therefore we all have the opportunity to pull from a unique archive for the raw materials we can use to create something new and unique. The question is not *"can"* you do it, it's *"will"* you?

## We want action

As I say in the beginning of my speech and book, *"Your Attitude for Success"*, the difference between those who succeed and those who don't is not ideas, it's action. Coming up with an idea doesn't make you any money. The only way you can profit from your ideas is to act on them. If you've ever seen a new product or service and said: *"I thought of that years ago"*, then you know what I mean. The reason you're seeing that product on a store shelf is due to the actions of one or many people. The reason it doesn't have your name on it is due to your inaction.

There's another analogy for this: *"If you're not the lead dog on the dogsled team... the view never changes."* So, what's it going to be for you? Are you going to keep doing the same things you've already done? Are you going to sit on a bunch of new ideas while someone else acts on them? Or, are you going to decide to evolve and grow, to take tangible steps to see your ideas come to fruition. I know you have it in you... do you?

## Thoughts and Ideas

_____

_____

_____

_____

_____

_____

_____

_____

_____

_____

_____

_____

_____

_____

_____

_____

_____

_____

_____

_____

_____

_____

_____

_____

# Are you living inside your comfort zone?

Whan's the last time you were outside your comfort zone? Last year? Last week? Today? We spend most of our time inside our comfort zones. Unless you're an adrenaline-junkie, you can't spend every day on the wild-side. That said, if you're not pushing yourself, you're putting a cap on your abilities, and your success. None of us know what we're capable of, until we try something new. It doesn't have to be something big. You don't have to go bungee jumping off a bridge in New Zealand, or skydiving. For some it's trying a new food. For others it's learning a new skill.

## Can you raise your prices?

When is the last time you raised your prices? I'll bet it seemed a little scary, didn't it? What if they all say No to the new price? But then, when the first customer says Yes to your new rate, it suddenly doesn't feel so scary. Fear of the unknown is natural. If you're not feeling a little uncomfortable about your new rates, they might not be high enough. A little price resistance shows you that you're probably at a good level. As long as enough people are saying Yes to fill your calendar, or at least your most popular dates, then you're probably in a good place. If everyone is saying Yes, without much resistance, then go higher.

## What's your Someday Isle?

I talk about Someday Isle in one of my books, and some of my presentations. Are you living there? You know, someday I'll go to Italy. Or, someday I'll write a book. Or, someday I'll go bungee jumping off that bridge in New Zealand. These are the things we put off, because we either think we don't have the time, or we're afraid to take the first step. I've been there. And then, when we actually do it, it's not so scary.

## Don't care what they'll think

I used to worry too much about what people might think if I went out on the dance floor and tried something new. Or what they would think if I failed. Let me let you in on a secret... most people could care less about your failures, or your successes. They're too focused on their own "stuff" to worry about yours. Most situations aren't life or death. So, what if you look silly on the dance floor. I'll bet you're having more fun than the people watching!

## Most successful people have failed more than you have

The road to success is rarely a straight line. Sure, the filtered version of people's success we see on social media often makes it seem that way, but there are few, true overnight success stories. Steve Jobs, Michael Jordan, and many "famous" people have failed their way to success. Muhammed Ali famously said (paraphrasing here) that it's not how many times you get knocked down, it's how many times you get back up, that matters. Each of us has our own bumpy, pothole filled road to where we are now. Mine includes health issues, getting downsized and more. What's yours? When you're living your own reality, you have to deal with what's in front of you, right now. I don't have to live your reality, and you don't have to live mine.

## I don't have the time

If I had a dollar for every time I put off doing something because I "didn't have the time" I'd be a very rich man. And then, one day, I realized that I can get lots of things, but more time isn't one of them. We're all racing through our lives, eating up 24 more hours, every day. Once you decide to get off Someday Isle, you find the time. Sure, you're really just taking it from one place and shifting it to another, but that's prioritizing. Have you ever changed a meeting, or put off some work, because a friend called with two tickets to the game, or concert or (fill in your own diversion)? You can change your priorities any time you want. They're yours to make and yours to change.

Our comfort zone isn't a static place. It's constantly changing. After all, once you do something that once seemed scary, it no longer seems so scary. You've expanded your comfort zone boundaries. Starting a business is scary. Hiring your first employee is scary. Asking out that cute guy or gal is scary. You don't do those things thinking you're going to fail. You plan to succeed. Sometimes it works out, sometimes it doesn't, but you keep going. You keep getting up.

## Are you ready to get uncomfortable?

Are you happy with the status quo? Not trying something new is akin to standing still. Every time I do consulting, or speak to wedding and event pros at a conference, I always hear complaining about new competitors. Are they trying new things? I'll bet they are. Are they disrupting the status quo? You bet. And, the more you're worried about them, the more disruptive power you're giving them. You can't be them, and they can't be you. What makes each of us who, and what we are, can't be copied. They can copy your marketing, website and list of services, but they have to deliver on them, and they're not you. All each of us can do is be our best selves. We can also push ourselves to achieve more. We can, in other words, get a little, or a lot uncomfortable. Are you ready?

# I

## Failure IS an option

Whether it's playing it safe, or being an over-protective parent, it's often tempting to try to reduce the chance for failure. After all, isn't failure bad? Actually, all failure isn't bad, because failure meant you tried something, and just didn't get the results you wanted. A speaker friend, Bruce Hale, once told me that: *"failure is just an unintended consequence."* He then went on to say that: *"success is often an unintended consequence as well,"* because we often get a successful result, just not the one that we had originally intended. You can't succeed, or fail, unless you try something new.

### What's the worst that can happen?

A few years back my friends and I went skydiving. We all got t-shirts after the jump that say: *"Skydiving – what's the worst that can happen?"* Now, with skydiving, there is a pretty bad possible outcome. Sure, it's not the one that we want, or expect to have, but it is possible. Yet, we went anyway. Why? I can't speak for my friends, but for me, that possible outcome wasn't even on my radar. I was thinking about the exhilaration, the rush and the views. There are many more people who will never go skydiving because of the possible outcome of failure – admittedly, a bad outcome.

So, are you motivated by the possibility of success, or debilitated by the fear of failure? Are you visualizing what it means to get the positive outcome you desire? Or, are you not even getting started because of the possibility that it won't work, and you won't end up where you want to go? What you should be asking yourself is: *"What's the worst that can happen?"* I once heard (or possibly read) that you should not only ask yourself what the worst possible outcome could be, you should also visualize that outcome. Is it really that scary? Would you be able to get through that challenge? Would you and your business, or family, be able to recover from that failure?

## You get what you focus on

Knowing and visualizing the worst-case scenario is not the same as focusing on it. You can't motivate yourself by avoiding negative outcomes. Imagine a catcher in a baseball game telling his or her pitcher: *"Whatever you do, don't pitch this next batter low and inside. Got it? Not low and inside or he'll hit it."* Where do you think that next pitch is going? Low and inside. A better approach would be to say: *"For this next batter, pitch it high and outside. That's a good pitch for him/her, high and outside."* Where do you think that pitch is going? More likely than not... high and outside, away from that batter's sweet spot.

## Where's your focus?

Are you focusing on the positive outcomes, trying new things, and acting upon your ideas? Or, are you not getting started because you can't stop seeing the worst-case scenarios? It's OK to know what that worst-case scenario is, just don't let it consume all of your attention. If he had focused on the failures, Thomas Edison wouldn't have tried 10,000 different ways to make a light bulb. If they had focused on the failure, 3M Corporation would never have created Post-It Notes. The adhesive they use for it was originally developed for another purpose, but it was a failure. Someone over there had the foresight to see another use for it, and viola, we have Post-It Notes.

## Lemons into Lemonade

You may have heard how some people can take a bad situation, and see the good, and they call it turning lemons into lemonade. The thing is, you have to be willing to get lemons in the first place. It's both our actions, and our inaction, that deliver the lemons to us. We may have been aiming for oranges, or apples, but instead we got lemons. When I wrote my first book, the original title was going to be: *"Insite."* I thought it was clever and that I could do a series, adding *"Hindsite"* and *"Foresite"* to it. Well, in my testing of the cover samples, the title fell like a lead balloon. It was either no reaction, or a negative one. However, I had also written on the cover, in small print: *"If your website was an employee, would you fire it?"* It was almost an afterthought, and I don't even remember how it ended up on the cover. When people looked at the cover samples, the title didn't move them, but that line did. So, even though I was told, by many people, that titles should be short and catchy, I went with: *"If your website was an employee, would you fire it?"* To this day, in its second edition, people still smile when they read or hear that title. That success was an unintended consequence.

## You got this

What have you tried, that didn't get you the outcome you originally wanted, but you made lemonade out of? What was your mindset that allowed you to see the success through the failure? And how can you channel that feeling, while understanding the risks, understanding the worst-case scenarios, and still take the actions necessary to succeed? You've already done it, probably countless times in your life. You took the chance, took the leap of faith, or simply didn't even consider the worst-case scenario at all. Don't sabotage your success with the fear of failure. Instead, nourish your success with the seeds of failure, so you can reap the rewards of success.

# First-world problems

The battery on my iPhone dies faster when I wear my Apple watch. That's a classic example of a "first-world problem". If you've never heard the expression, a "first-world problem" is something that a person in a third-world (developing world) country would never say, and probably wouldn't understand. People who are wondering if they're going to eat today aren't worried about having "nothing good to watch on TV tonight".

When I first visited Mumbai, India, I was struck by the close proximity of poverty and wealth. I travel a lot, and I see both poverty and wealth, but never intermingled the way it is there. In most major cities, the poverty and wealth are separated. You can tell when you're in a wealthy area, and you can tell when you're not. But not in Mumbai. As you ride from one place, to another, you pass 5-star hotels, and extreme poverty, almost randomly. New apartment buildings rise next to ramshackle huts, protected only by tin roofs and plastic sheeting.

## Mixed emotions

On my second time to Mumbai I again felt mixed emotions. On the one-hand, I feel very lucky to have been born where I was, to these particular parents. I wasn't born with a silver spoon in my mouth, but I've also never known poverty or real hunger. On the other hand, I also feel guilty when I'm there. I get to go back home to my first-world problems, including the flight delays and expensive airport food.

## It's all about perspective

When my younger son was turning 16, I wanted to try to explain to him just how fortunate we are to live where we do, and to have the opportunities we have. We decided to volunteer for Habitat for Humanity, as we both love to use tools and build things. We didn't go to a third-world country, we went to Omaha, Nebraska. Omaha is a very nice city, and not one I that you'd automatically associate with poverty. I had been going there for many years, for business, and had only really seen middle-America. The unemployment rate was relatively low, new houses were popping up and old buildings were being revitalized into condos, restaurants and shops.

## Where has this been?

So, I was very surprised to see the neighborhood change as we drove to the Habitat offices. You see, I had never had a reason to go to North Omaha. The offices were out west, where the new construction was happening. North Omaha has boarded up houses. It has gang violence. Who knew? Certainly not me, since I didn't live there. It wasn't like Mumbai, with the poverty intertwined with the affluence. My son was surprised to see people going into the boarded-up house next to our build site. We were both surprised to hear the stories from the Habitat staff, about a single mother, living with her children in a basement apartment, with dirt floors. This wasn't the 1800's, it was the 2000's. We ended up doing Habitat, 3 years in a row, in Omaha; before he headed off to college – and all of the first-world problems that come with it.

## Why am I telling you this?

As humans, we tend to reflect on our triumphs, and failures. I hope you've had both, I know I have. Both triumphs and failures come from opportunities and taking action. You can't have either unless you try something. Yes, sometimes bad things happen, to good people (like health issues and car accidents, both of which I've had). Proactive people aren't luckier than the rest of us. Proactive people aren't sitting around waiting for someone, or something, to improve their situation. Proactive people are acting on their ideas, not sitting on them. As I said in another chapter, failure isn't a bad thing. It's just an unintended consequence of trying something, and not getting the result you desired.

## "I've never made a bad decision. I've just had bad results."

I love that quote by William Greenblatt. None of us has a do-over button. We can't go back in time and make a different decision. All we can do is learn from it, and make better decisions going forward. Successful people don't stop trying new things when they experience a failure. They don't give up when they hit a road block. They persevere, and that's why they succeed.

## I wish you lots of first-world problems

So, my wish for you is that you have lots of first-world problems. I hope they run out of your favorite dessert in the restaurant. I hope the battery dies on your phone when you need to take one more photo. I hope it's a little too cold in your house, and you have to put another blanket on the bed. Why? Because if those are the worst of your problems, you're doing fine. I look forward to hearing your stories of success, and yes, your stories of failure. Let's toast to them both!

## Thoughts and Ideas

_____

_____

_____

_____

_____

_____

_____

_____

_____

_____

_____

_____

_____

_____

_____

_____

_____

_____

_____

_____

_____

_____

_____

# HOW EMOTIONS AFFECT YOUR BUSINESS DECISIONS

In preparing for another new presentation for Wedding MBA, in Las Vegas, I did research and a survey about emotional decision-making. The original concept for the presentation was "Why do entrepreneurs make emotional decisions?" The more I got into my research, the more it became clear that all decisions involve emotions on some level, they just may not appear to be the primary driver of your decisions.

Antonio Demasio is arguably the world's leading expert on emotional decision making. His TED Talk has had over 1 million views. He's found that people who have damage to the part of their brain that controls emotions have difficulty making even the most basic of decisions; what to wear, what to eat, etc. Therefore, all decisions involve some level of emotions.

## How or Why?

So, what we need to be asking is "how", rather than "why" emotions affect our decisions. It's easy to recall when strong emotions have swayed our decisions, usually in a bad way. Most decisions made when angry or upset end up having some negative implications. The ones you wish you could take back. Scientists tell us that we tend to focus on the negative consequences, rather than the positive. They seem to take root more deeply in our memories, and we use those negative memories to make current and future decisions to try to avoid those same negative consequences, again.

## Emotions, Pricing and Negotiating

Since many, if not most of you reading this own, or run a small business, your personal identity and your business identity are closely connected. When someone questions your pricing, or tries to get a discount, many people react emotionally, as if it's an attack on your value. While that's a common reaction, it's a little misguided. When you're the customer, don't you want to have both the best quality/service and the right price? You don't want to overpay. You want to know that someone else isn't going to come along after you and pay less, for the same services. You are entitled to ask for the best price. So are your clients.

## The power of NO

If you've heard any of the webinars I've done on sales, or heard me present on sales at a conference, you've heard me speak about the power of "No." It's a very powerful word. They have the right to ask for a better price. You have the right to say No. Don't deny them that right. They won't know that they have your best price until you say No. When you look at the situation differently, and don't take offense to them asking (that's the emotional part), you can make a better, more definitive decision.

## How do you say No?

Here's how I like to say No, while showing them that I still want to work with them: *"I can appreciate you asking, and I know that you want to know that you're getting the best price, for the services you want and need. You also want to know that someone else isn't going to pay less, for those same services. That's why I don't negotiate my rates. Everyone gets the same price, for the same services, because you all want, and deserve, the best quality and service."* And then ask for the sale, as asking for a discount is a very strong buying signal.

## Negotiating vs. Discounting

In most cases I prefer a policy of discounting, but not negotiating. Discounting is when, based upon a predetermined set of products, services, or conditions, there is a discount available. For instance, if someone buys your lowest package or service, there is no discount available. But if they buy more, for instance a higher package, there is a discount built in versus buying those same services individually. If people can buy more than one of your products or services, you may decide to offer a volume discount. However, anyone else buying the same things, would get the same discount.

Negotiating is like the Wild West, with different people paying different prices, for the same services or products. The challenge is that people talk. These days they talk online, sharing their conquests and prices. Unless you're prepared to defend giving one customer a better price than another, for the same things, negotiating is a slippery slope. It actually is empowering to remove negotiating from your business vocabulary. When you know you can't give them a better price, you defend the value, instead of the price. You can say No, and mean it. Say it nicely, but say it.

## And if they insist...

How do you tell them No, when they keep asking? Here's what I like to say: *"If price is the most important factor when choosing your (venue, photographer, band, DJ, planner...) then I'm probably not the right fit for your wedding. Couples like you don't choose us because we're the cheapest. Couples like you choose us because they want to trust one of the most important day in their lives, to someone who's going to deliver everything they want, and more... someone who's going to go above and beyond to make their wedding a success. That's what we can, and will do for you, just as we do for dozens of other couples, every year. If you read our reviews you won't see them saying 'I'm glad they were the cheapest', they're saying 'Our wedding was better than we ever dreamed it would be'"...* and ask for the sale!

## Emotions and Reviews

It's not hard to see how reviews can come into play with reviews. When you get a really good review, you feel great. When someone says something that's not as favorable, you feel bad. You often take it as a personal attack, even when they aren't mentioning you by name. WeddingWire and I have done webinars on reviews, including how to handle and respond to negative comments, so I'm not going to rehash all of those here, but suffice it to say that you need to take a step back, consult someone who's not emotionally connected to the situation, and then do the right thing.

## Take a deep breath...

Don't respond when you're upset. Don't click "Reply" until you've taken a step back, analyzed the situation and until you understand the consequences, current and future, of your actions. Trying to prove that you're right, is trying to prove the customer wrong. Any time you try to prove a customer wrong, you lose. Often you need to swallow your pride and make the right, long-term decision. How would you counsel a good friend to respond if it were their business?

Don't fight your emotions, embrace them. You made a very emotional decision to start your business, or to get into your industry. Respect that and trust your emotions to guide you to success. Just understand that there is a right time and platform for your decisions. Things look a lot clearer on the other side of a decision. Learn from your past decisions and you'll learn to do the right thing.

## Thoughts and Ideas

---
---
---
---
---
---
---
---
---
---
---
---
---
---
---
---
---
---
---
---
---
---
---
---
---

# How full is your glass?

There's an old joke: *The optimist sees the glass as half-full. The pessimist sees the glass as half-empty. The engineer sees the glass as twice as large as is needed for this application!* I'm an optimist. I suppose I always have been and like most of you, I've had my share of things in my life to give pause to that attitude. I'm not a Pollyanna, someone who is blindly optimistic regardless of the situation or facts. I'm definitely a realist, but I also prefer to see, or seek the good. I prefer to look for solutions rather than to dwell on the problem. Complaining rarely fixes the problem by itself. We need action to do that.

## Business is terrible, while business is great – huh?

I have the opportunity to interact with many, many wedding and event pros each year, both domestically and internationally. One question I like to ask is: *"How's business?"* It's interesting to me to hear: *"Business is great"* and *"Business is bad"* in the same market, by people in the same category and around the same price point. Some of this is reflecting how they're doing compared to their projections. Some is due to expectations. And some is due to comparisons. One caterer might be doing 50 weddings this year and consider it a banner year. Another could be doing 50 and consider it a failure. One officiant could be getting two to three times what a similar officiant charges and be filling their calendar, while the lower-priced one complains that he or she can't close a sale.

## The more things change, the more they remain the same.

I've been hearing this same tale of woe for the over 25 years I've been in this industry. One business complaining about how bad things are while another is thriving. Is it just their attitude? Are they just the glass-half-full people? No, but that doesn't hurt. Your attitude will be transmitted to your prospects and clients, in-person, on the phone and through your digital communications. We all want to do business with people who truly want our business and are interested in giving us the positive results we desire. If they seem indifferent as to whether they get your business or not, it's way too easy to find another option. It's not different when you're the customer or the supplier.

## There's more to it than pricing.

Your customers are shopping for more than just the best price. They're shopping for the best experience. That experience starts with their first interaction with your business and brand. Your ads, your social presence, your website and yes, the way you communicate with them, all send signals – to stay or to flee. The lower price won't work if they don't feel confident that you'll deliver the results they want. The lowest price only wins *after* they've determined that they're going to get what they want and need. No one wants to overpay, but getting a better price and inferior results is not a good bargain.

## How full do they see your glass?

Whether you call it the "Law of Attraction" or you've watched and agree with "The Secret" video, ultimately we are how we're perceived by others. What are you projecting to your customers and prospects? Do they feel attracted to you, or repelled? We all know someone who is like a magnetic field, drawing us in with their energy. We feel good when we're around them. We feel empowered by them. And we want to take in more of their positivity whenever we can. Conversely, we also all know people who seem to suck the life out of us (I have a feeling that right now you're smiling and thinking of someone – not in a good way). We dread being around them because they can bring down your good moods. They find the negative in almost any situation. They can't see the glass as half-anything because they'll complain about the glass itself!

### Hit the reset button.

I've said in my books, sales training and presentations that you need to hit the reset button before every call, email or meeting. The last interaction you had with a client or colleague has nothing to do with the next one... that is, unless it went really well, and then you want to bring that positivity with you. Why the last customer bought, or didn't buy, has nothing to do with the needs and wants of the next one. If you bring that baggage with you, you're not going to be actively listening. You're going to make incorrect assumptions (and you know what they say about when you assume, right?). If you want to know what's going to help this customer to buy, you're going to need to hit that reset button and start with a clean slate.

### It may be the thousandth time you've said it...

...but it's likely the first time *they're* hearing it. If you don't have the same conviction in your voice, and show excitement about the opportunity to work with them, they'll find someone else who will. Remember that by the time you get a chance to communicate with them, they've put you on their short list of prospects. They've already eliminated most of your competition and they already think you're a good fit. Prove them right by actively listening, and they'll reward you by telling you what you need to know to make the sale. Prove them wrong by making assumptions about what they want and talking too much instead of listening, and they'll go away, never to be heard from again.

## Treat your business like a bamboo plant.

I've heard that it takes 5 years of watering and feeding the seeds of the bamboo plant until it breaks ground. Once it breaks ground it grows very fast (it's a member of the Grass Family of plants). It takes a lot of patience and optimism to keep watering and feeding the plant when you can't see it growing. It's the same with your business. You need to be planting seeds, watering and feeding them, even when you're not seeing any growth. Your advertising, your social presence, your networking and your sales process are like the planting, watering and feeding of the seeds. You don't always see the results right away. But if you don't do those things you won't see the results at all. There's another old saying: *"When is the best time to plant a tree? 20 years ago! When is the next best time to plant a tree? Today!"*

## Do the work, trust the process.

My uncle, who just turned 90, is still a life-coach. I guess you have good credibility when you've lived that long! When my business as an independent speaker, consultant and sales trainer was in its infancy, I was pressing ahead at full speed. About 18 months into my new venture my uncle told me: *"You're pushing too hard. Pull back and let it come to you."*

I reflected on his words and realized that if I had been planting the right seeds, watering and feeding them, I would start to see the results. What I had been doing was trying to force the business, trying to make something out of nothing, where no seed had been planted. When I heeded his advice, and kept watering and feeding, nurturing the relationships and platforms I had already invested in, my business increased 40% the following year! And every time since, when I've felt a little desperation from a hole in my calendar or felt like I was pushing too hard, I've pulled back. And, lo and behold, the email inquiries came in, the phone rang and the social interactions have led to new business. Take some time to make sure you're nurturing the seeds you've been planting. Make sure you haven't let some relationships wither and die. Go to that networking event. Check in with your industry friends. Be proactive. Follow up with your inquiries until you get a yes, or a no. And most importantly, embrace your glass. It's as full as you want it to be!

## Thoughts and Ideas

# How to be the experienced wedding pro, without sounding old

I had the privilege of speaking at a national conference about a touchy subject... getting older. Why is it a touchy subject, after all aging is inevitable? As a matter of fact, getting older beats the alternative (dying young)! The reason it's touchy is because in our industry, wedding pros, like you, get older every year, while your target market, engaged couples, stay about the same age. In my over 25 years around this industry couples have only gotten about 5 years older, while I've added those 25 years to my total (that's not fair, but it's true).

## So, what's the problem?

Actually I don't think there is a problem, but for many wedding pros it can become an issue. At a certain point you find yourself the age of the parents of your clients, while you need to relate to the couple and understand their needs. Any of you who have children know that relating to your kids is not as easy as relating to people your own age. And therein lies the issue, or does it?

As with many other of life's issues there are many ways to see this. Do you need to be the age of your couples to relate to them? I don't think so. You just need to work to understand their needs as it relates to your business and service. You also need to constantly adapt to the way they want to do business.

## Technology changes all the time

One of the most fundamental ways our market has changed over the past 10 to 20 years is the advent of email, and other forms of digital communication. For many, if not most of you, getting a prospect on the phone is your preferred first method of contact. But, we all know that doesn't happen these days and email is, and will continue to be the way they reach out to us for the foreseeable future. It's not up to us to try to change them, it's up to us to adapt. A basic rule of business is to communicate with your customers using their preferred technology. If they email you, email them back. If they call you, call them back.

## Don't make a problem where there is none

The key is to not highlight something that may not be an issue. Don't do and say things that get them thinking you may be out of touch (by the way, any of us can be out of touch, regardless of our age). Don't say things like: *"When I was your age..."* or *"My kids are your age..."* or *"My grandchildren..."*. For example, I used to talk about how long I've been married, but now I just say I've been happily married for a long time (my wife wasn't happy about me omitting the number of years until I explained why – and if asked I'll certainly say how many years). I used to say how old my two sons are, but now I just say I have two Gen Y sons.

## How many year's experience is enough?

Do you really need to say you've been in business *"since 1992"* on your marketing? Is that relevant to your prospects? What they care most about is what you're doing now, not what you did 10, 15 or 20 years ago. Is having 5 years experience better than 1? Probably. Is having 10 years experience better than 5? Maybe. Is having

20 years experience better than 15? Hard to say, isn't it. It's not the number of years, it's what you did in those years that matters. One wedding pro could have done 5 weddings per year, for 10 years, for a total of 50 weddings. Another may have done 30 weddings per year, for 5 years, for a total of 150 weddings. So you can see that the number doesn't tell the whole story.

## It's not just your words, it's your actions and marketing

I've often said that you don't always get credit for doing things right, but you often lose points for getting it wrong. One of the most glaring things you can do is to have an AOL or Hotmail email address for your business (yes, I still see those on business cards). If you have a website, which I would hope all of you do, then your email should be yourname@yourwebsite.com, regardless of your age. If you're 25 and using a Gmail address, I would tell you the same thing. Can you think of any major company that uses AOL, Gmail or Yahoo email addresses (other than employees of AOL, Google or Yahoo)? No, of course not. Using anything other than your website for your email can make you look less professional, less serious, not full time or like you're a startup, to some clients. It's easy and inexpensive to set this up. Just ask the company that hosts your website, I'm sure they have email for you there as well. I just set up a new website and it was less than $50 per year for an exchange server email (so I can use Outlook). Having your email at your website won't get them to pat you on the back, but you won't lose points for it.

## What's your first impression?

Having outdated branding, business cards, logo and most of all your website, can hurt you as well. Most of our customers will see our websites before we get to meet them, so keep it up to date, not just in content, but in design. The same goes for your social media presence. Know which platforms your clients are using and learn how to get a better return from your investment in time and money.

It's not about trying to dress young, or talking young. It's about staying relevant with your work and being open to adapting to a changing market, because the market is always changing. In the years I've been around the wedding and event industry I've seen lots of change. The wedding pros I know who've been in the industry that long, and are thriving, are doing things a lot different than they did 25 years ago, are you? If you're getting a lot of resistance from your prospects the place to look first is in the mirror. For most of our businesses the biggest hurdle is found there. Then take a look at what others are doing, network with younger wedding pros (mentoring can be helpful for both of you) and listen and watch for new trends, not just in your skillset, but business and marketing trends. You don't have to be the first to jump on them, but if you don't know they exist it's easier to be left behind. I look forward to hearing your stories of success, no matter how long you've been in business.

# I'D RATHER BE HAPPY AND SUCCESSFUL, THAN RIGHT

When I speak about handling reviews I encourage you to write replies to all reviews, good and bad. Write them for the people who will be reading them (as opposed to the person who wrote them). And, don't get into a he-said she-said about a bad review, in public. When you have an upset customer it's always best to keep that discussion offline, and out of email if you can. Your goal is to make your customer happy, so they'll refer you and, if you offer more than just wedding services, maybe come back and use you again.

One of my favorite things to live by is that: *"I've learned in business, and in life, that I'd rather be happy and successful, than be right."* If I have to prove that I'm right, that means someone else has to be wrong. If I tell my wife that she's wrong about something, how is that going to work out for me? If I tell a customer that they're wrong, how is that going to work out for me? (just as poorly!)

## Long term value

The long-term value of a customer relationship is the amount of money that you will earn over the life of that relationship. When a customer has a problem, that long-term value gets paused, not stopped. If you handle their issue, quickly, and to their satisfaction, the long-term value not only continues, it could be higher. Customers will usually forgive you getting something wrong, as long as you make it right, quickly. Some of my best customer and industry relationships are with people who first came to me with a problem. After handling it professionally, and quickly, they knew that if something else should arise, I would take care of it quickly and professionally as well. Their 'problem' was really an opportunity.

## Give until it hurts

I've heard countless examples of wedding pros who have offered customers more than would seem warranted to make them happy, and then they were rewarded with referral business, possibly more referral business than they would have gotten had nothing gone wrong. I know the owner of a DJ company who has 7 DJ's. He calls every customer on Monday morning, if he wasn't personally at their event, to see how things went for them. On one Monday, he called a mother who had hired their company to DJ her young son's birthday party. The woman expressed that she wasn't happy with the performance of the DJ. He listened, apologized (one of the most important things to do) and then offered her a partial refund. She appeared to be satisfied... but he wasn't. So, he went to a toy store and bought a gift card and note card. He hand-wrote an apology in the notecard, something to the effect of: *"I'm sorry that everything wasn't exactly the way you had expected for your son's party. Please buy him a gift from us."* and put the gift card in the envelope with it. He hand-delivered the envelope to her house. Within two weeks he had gotten two referrals from her that booked him for events. A few months later he called to tell me he had heard that I was telling his story. I asked if he wanted me to not tell it anymore and he said: *"No, it's fine, I just wanted you to know that I have now booked 3 jobs now from that, not two!"*

## Satisfaction Guaranteed!

Another wedding pro told me that his company has a 100% satisfaction guarantee. A groom called after his wedding to say that something hadn't gone correctly. After listening, an apologizing, the owner asked the groom where to send the refund check. The groom said: *"You don't have to give us back all of the money."* But the wedding pro reiterated that they have a 100%, money-back guarantee, and since everything wasn't to their satisfaction they were refunding the entire amount. The wedding pro told me that they, too, had gotten at least two referrals who booked them from that couple. I asked him if anyone abused their 100% satisfaction guarantee and complained, even if nothing went wrong? He said: *"You would think they might, but it hasn't happened, at least not yet."*

## Thinking long-term

Both of these examples show how a little short-term pain, giving the refunds, can lead to long-term gain. Had they not handled their situations well it could have led to poor reviews, which could have cost them other business. I once had a wedding DJ approach me at a conference to tell me the story of a wedding where the power had gone out (not his fault). The couple went to the DJ at the event and demanded a refund. The DJ wasn't an owner and had no authority to give a refund. It's certainly questionable as to whether a refund was due, given the situation. The DJ would have kept playing but the wedding couldn't have gone on without power. Even if he had backup power for his equipment, the venue didn't have backup power and sent everyone home. The customer wrote an email to the owner of the DJ company demanding a refund, and threatened to post 1-star reviews online if he didn't comply. Instead of taking a deep breath, trying to put himself in their shoes (their wedding was ruined), thinking about the possible consequences and trying to appease the customer, he wrote them back a stern email saying that no refund was warranted as it wasn't his fault the power went out. The customer went and posted the negative reviews, exactly as they had said (or threatened). Now, the owner of the DJ company was standing before me asking how he could make those bad reviews go away. I asked him how much he would be willing to pay to erase them. Was it more than they paid him for the wedding? He said: *"Absolutely"*. I said: *"So, now you're willing to pay that much, why not when they first came to you?"*

## Doing the right thing

He let his emotions get the best of him. Yes, they were bordering on extortion, and unfairly targeting him. He called their bluff and he lost. Had he called me before writing back to them I would have told him to think long-term, not short-term. I hope this never happens to you, but if it does, remember that you have an unhappy customer, and your first mission is to make them happy. Try to see it from their side, as if you were the customer. Think about what you would you want to happen, and then act appropriately.

# Just like starting over

I'm a new speaker. That's a funny way for a Certified Speaking Professional® (CSP), who's been speaking professionally for years, to start an article. I've taken a giant leap backwards in my speaking career. I'm a CSP and (as of this writing) one of only 33 Global Speaking Professionals in the world, but I'm also a beginner. Some of you already know that I have committed to becoming conversationally fluent in Spanish. I was at a conference in Mexico, and I thought that my high school Spanish would allow me to engage in basic conversation. Well, I was wrong. High school was a very long time ago, and I realize now how little Spanish I had actually learned.

## When in Rome (or Cancun)

I came to the realization that when a foreigner comes to the US, we expect them to speak English. And when we go to their country, we also expect them to speak English. That's not right. I wanted to respect the people in the other country by at least trying to have a conversation in their language. Once I started to get better, I was encouraged to keep going.

Everywhere I went I tried to practice speaking Spanish. Whether it was with a waiter in a restaurant, a taxi driver, or a conference attendee. If I knew, or sensed that someone was fluent in Spanish, I would try to at least exchange a few words, or sentences. I was able to speak Spanish in many places, including Ireland, Dubai, Australia and even India. Did I get things wrong? Yup! But I kept plugging away.

## You did what?

Then, in January 2016 (about 3 years after starting), I took a leap of faith and committed to give a presentation in Spanish in September. Yes, September of the same year! I was nowhere near ready in January, but it gave me a target date, and 8 months, to get ready. I worked on my Spanish throughout those months, but not specifically the speech. I figured there would be time as I got closer for that. Then in June, a funny thing happened. I was invited to speak in Uruguay in August. Uh oh, there goes a month off my timeline!

## Shhh, it's a surprise

I was going to present 3 times, twice in English and once in Spanish (which would be a surprise to the attendees). For the Spanish presentation I chose one of my more popular topics: *"The Price Is Right,"* which is about how to handle the "How much do you charge?" question, and pricing on your website. It's a subject I know well, which I figured would help. Well, at least I thought it would help. It wasn't just a new language I was trying to learn; it was also a vocabulary of words that don't usually come up in casual conversation.

When I learned that I had a long layover in Panama, a friend arranged for me to present to a small group of local wedding pros, which would be my rehearsal for Uruguay. I practiced the speech over, and over. I would record myself and then listen to the recording when I was driving, walking through an airport, and exercising. The words became more familiar, but still not second nature.

I reverted back to using my iPad mini for my speaking notes (something I've mostly abandoned when presenting in English).

When it came time to present in Panama, I was very nervous. I had the jitters like a beginning speaker. It was partly because I wanted to do well, and partly because it was so different from where I am as a professional speaker (in English). I was mostly reading as I presented, which seemed to bother me more than my audience. They were very appreciative that I had even tried to present in Spanish, and gave me great feedback.

## It's like a whole other country

Two days later I was in Montevideo, Uruguay. But now, instead of a dozen in my audience, it was 140 people. They had told me there would be a translator for me, as I was the only non-native Spanish speaker. The rest were from countries in Central and South America, as well as Mexico. I've presented with a translator before, but this time was different. Instead of being a simultaneous translation, where the attendees have wireless earphones to hear the translation, in real time, this conference had a consecutive translation. I would speak a few lines, and then the translator, who was sitting on a chair in front of the audience, would speak the translation into his microphone. While he did a great job keeping the meaning and emotion, It completely ruined the flow and energy for me, and I felt, for the audience.

## Time for another leap of faith

The next morning, I was to give another presentation in English, and then my surprise Spanish presentation to close the conference. I decided that it would be better to try to present the second one in Spanish, than to use the consecutive translation. So, that afternoon, I enlisted the help of two new friends from Chile and

Venezuela, to help me translate the speech. It took us a couple of hours to get it right.

And then, the next morning, I shook off the nervousness and stood in front of the audience and asked them if it would be OK if I tried to present this one in Spanish. There was a thunderous applause. And off I went, mostly reading (as I hadn't had time to practice the way I had with 'The Price is Right'). I wasn't able to ad-lib or go off-script much, if at all. That takes time. That takes practice. That takes a level of comfort with both the material, and the vocabulary. That's why I'm a beginner, again. It's a humbling experience, but also quite exciting and liberating. It's easy to get comfortable, and maybe you can relate, with that comfort can also come a little complacency, or boredom. So, what are you doing that's new and exciting? What are you trying that makes you feel a little like a beginner? Join me in stepping backward, the first step on taking a giant leap forward.

**AUTHOR'S NOTE:** *As of this writing I've presented in 5 countries in Spanish. My personal goal is to do one of my books as an audio book in Spanish. That's going to take more practice, but I'm confident I'll get there, someday!*

# NONE OF US IS AN EXPERT
## AT EVERYTHING

I was once conducting a mastermind group in the UK for 10 DJ companies, who have varying years of experience (from 5 years to almost 40 years). What stood out to me was that this group, who all have good, successful companies, each have different business skills. Their technical (computer/internet/website) expertise ranged from low to very high. That's to be expected with any group. What I didn't expect is that one of the companies, who's not known for his technical expertise when it comes to websites, was chiming in to help the group with some pretty technical features of Google Analytics. Quite a few of the guys in the room, including me (as I've consulted with him privately), were very surprised.

It turns out that he had been studying up, using websites and YouTube videos, and had picked up a few new tricks – and I'll have to admit, I didn't even know one or two of them. A couple of the guys in the room are pretty well skilled in making websites, including his, so they were even more surprised. That got me thinking that each of us has our own history, knowledge and skillset. None of us is an expert in everything, and we shouldn't assume what others may, or may not know. We have our own, unique expertise that comes from the combined knowledge we've gleaned, and that knowledge is unique to each of us.

## We're each a product of our history

Many wedding pros have transitioned into their own businesses after leaving corporate, or technical jobs. They may have deep knowledge of software such as Microsoft Excel or Outlook. While others struggle to make a basic spreadsheet, they're knocking out detailed reports with ease. However, those same people who have no problem using Excel might struggle with other areas of their businesses (i.e. marketing, design, websites, etc.). *None of us is an expert at everything.* When presented with a need for our business, we always have the choice of doing something ourselves, or hiring a professional. Knowing when to choose each path is something we often have to learn by trial and error.

It's often easier to try to learn a new skill or software program, instead of hiring someone to do that task for you, especially when funds are tight. When you realize that the time you're investing in learning that skill is time away from building your business, or away from your family, often the right answer is to hire the professional – after all, isn't that why we want them to hire us? If you're new at a skill, it's going to take time for you to master it. If it's a skill that you can profit from, maybe it's worth investing in the training and time. For others, hiring an outside specialist is a jump-start to that professional level. What's that worth to you?

## When is it time to make the switch?

I realized that when I switched from doing my own taxes, to hiring a professional CPA. My dad is a retired CPA and we would do my taxes together (my degree is in marketing and accounting). However, he's been retired for a long time, so he's not up on the latest tax laws and software. I never practiced accounting, so even though I have a good understanding, I wasn't up on the latest info, either. So, a few years ago I hired an accountant, and the first year he did my taxes he showed me deductions I hadn't been taking and was able to recoup some refunds from prior years. In other words, he paid for himself the first time I used him.

Too many of us fall into the trap of thinking that because we have expertise in one area, it's automatically transferrable to another skill. We're comfortable with using a computer, so we think we can make our own website. We're creative, so we think we can design our own marketing collateral. It's understandable, especially when you consider that most of us started as, or still are, small businesses, where you, the owner, is wearing many hats. When you're boot-strapping a new business, you usually do everything yourself. As a matter of fact, Sam Walton, the founder of Wal-Mart, is purported to have said (and I'm paraphrasing): *"When I started my business, I knew I'd be wearing a lot of hats. I just didn't realize I'd be wearing them all at the same time."*

## Time is slipping away

An important realization, in any business, is learning to value your time. It's the one thing you'll never get any more of. Sometimes it's best to hire someone to do something you do have the skill for, just because your time is better spent on other tasks. I put off hiring an assistant for a couple of years. I knew it would be helpful, but I wasn't sure I could justify the expense. Everything was getting done, but at what cost? The cost was my time, sitting on the sofa at night with my laptop, working, when I should have been spending time with my family, or even just relaxing.

What's your time worth? What else could you be doing if you delegated some tasks to someone else (virtual assistant, intern, employee)? None of us is an expert at everything, no matter how long, or short, you've been in business. Sometimes we all need help. Becoming aware of that is the first step to accomplishing more, achieving more and profiting more.

# THE LURE OF THE 'FRIENDOR'

I'm pretty handy with a set of tools, and I've often helped out a friend or relative with a repair or home improvement project. In other words, I've been a 'friendor.' Have you? A friendor is a friend or relative who performs a service that could have otherwise been provided by paying an individual or business. It happens all the time. Have you ever benefitted from the services of a friend or relative? I'll bet you have. When it works out well, you just smile and move on. When it doesn't, you have to decide whether to pay someone to complete or fix the job, or look to another friendor to do so.

## Not all friendors are created equally

While most, or all of us have either been or benefitted from this arrangement, not all friendors are the same. Some, like me, aren't currently professionals in that skill. In my case, I'm not currently a general contractor, although I did work as one earlier in my life. I have the skills to do many of the jobs that a practicing professional would do. So, whether I do something in my house, or for my friend, relative, neighbor or in-law, it will get done at a level on par with at least some of the practicing professionals (maybe better than some, maybe worse).

Have you ever helped a friend or relative with services for which you would normally charge? Many of the folks I've met in the industry started out that way. Maybe you were an art student and you took the photos for a friend's wedding, party, family or new baby. You were skilled in the craft, you just didn't charge. Did it work out well for both sides (they were happy with your work, and you were happy to give them that gift)?

## Learning on the job

Other times a friendor is learning that craft of skill 'on the job', which is to say on the wedding or event. That's where the trouble can come in. Giving your professional services at no charge still avails the recipient with professional services. Learning how to arrange floral centerpieces, bake and decorate a wedding cake or keep the flow going with the right music should not be happening leading up to, or during a real  wedding or event... at least I wouldn't want it happening on my wedding or event, would you?

## Are friendors your competition?

We, in the industry, know all too well that it's a slippery slope using friendors for a wedding. Being a skilled photographer doesn't mean you know where to be looking, or what's going to happen next at a wedding. The skills that make you the envy of your friends in the kitchen at dinner parties, aren't the same as the ones that you need to create meals for 200 guests, and get them all out quickly, hot and plated the same way. Cooking for 2, or even 12, isn't the same as cooking for 200.

In another chapter (CraigsList is not your competitor) I wrote that if the couple has a very low budget, then you were never a real possibility for them. There will always be lower-priced competitors. As a matter of fact, many of you reading this were the lower-priced competitor when you started. If you were a friendor before becoming a paid professional, were you taking away a possible sale from a pro at that time? Maybe yes, maybe no. I've also written and spoken about how we're all hypocrites for asking about price, or for a discount when we're the customer, and then complaining when our customers ask first about price, or ask for a discount from us. We can't have it both ways. If you've ever been, or used a friend/relative instead of paying a professional, you can't complain when a couple chooses to use one.

## And the problem is...?

The problem is not that they use friendors. The problem is when they use friendors and it doesn't go well: the friend who misses the important photos; the cake that doesn't look or taste the way they wanted; the friend who stops performing their service and starts acting like a guest. Those are the problems.

There are opportunities to help prevent this. Some businesses have popped up serving the DIY couple and their friendors. Whether it's selling them the supplies they need, with instructions, teaching courses or giving them an instruction manual/ guide book, some wedding and event pros are servicing this market, helping to minimize the nightmares. Notice I said minimize, and not eliminate. People are people, and many will bite off more than they can chew, get in over their heads and fail miserably. Let's just hope it doesn't happen to anyone you know.

## Now what?

Just as you shouldn't waste too much energy on trying to sell your services, at your prices, to DIY couples and those who are looking to CraigsList for cheap vendors, don't waste too much time or energy on those who are choosing friendors. Yes, you can try to educate them. Yes, collect every article, blog and posting you can find from couples who have had horrible experiences with friendors. You can't make them read those things and you can't change their minds if they believe that will never happen to them. Move on and place your efforts in marketing to your real, core audience, improving your website and increasing your sales conversions. That's a much better use of your time and effort.

# Wanna get lucky?

OK, get your minds out of the gutter (you know who you are) and let's talk about luck as it pertains to your business. The Roman philosopher, Seneca, is credited with the saying: *"Luck Is What Happens When Preparation Meets Opportunity."* You need both of these to 'get lucky'; however, the preparation part comes first. Or, as my friend David Rothstein recently told me: *"It takes 20 years to become an overnight success!"* You have to do the work, learn the skills, invest in your success, and then, be on the lookout for opportunity.

## Life is a highway

If your life path has been like mine, it hasn't been a straight line. Far from it. Mine is a series of zigs and zags, fueled by opportunities. You've probably heard the expression *"being in the right place, at the right time."* Well, I believe that we're all right where we're supposed to be, all the time. Opportunity is all around us. That's why some businesses are succeeding, while others - in the same market and category - are faltering or failing. Whether it's opting to pass on opportunities, or not seeing them, the result is still the same. Nothing ventured, nothing gained.

Your competitors aren't getting lucky. They're simply seeing, or seizing, opportunities that you didn't. We all can get blinded by our day to day obligations. Our ability to see the opportunities is overshadowed by answering email, taking the kids to school and paying the bills. The easiest thing to do is to keep your blinders on, and avoid the opportunities. Why? Because, taking action requires time, and money, and personal capital. What will others think of you? How will this affect your family, and current customers? etc.

## You can't connect the dots looking forward

If you haven't already seen it, I recommend that you watch Steve Jobs' commencement address at Stanford University, in 2005. It's often called the 'connect the dots' speech. He talks about how we can't connect the dots in our lives looking forward. However, looking back, we can see how each step led to the next. That's my life in a nutshell. Looking back, my seemingly unrelated 'dots' have clearly led to one another. Whether they were 'sales-related' dots, or personal dots, they clearly connect in hindsight.

What I've found is that I don't actively look for the next 'dot'. Rather, I go about my days knowing that opportunities will present themselves. I don't know where, and I don't know when, I just know that - as they have in the past - they will appear. I don't want to get all 'new-age' on you, but as I mentioned in another chapter, my uncle once told me that I was pushing too hard. He said to pull back on my availability, and let it come to me. I wasn't immediately sure what he meant, but over time it became clearer. I can feel when I'm trying too hard. I feel the resistance. But, when I pull back, I can feel the attraction.

## You gotta believe

Now, whether you believe in a universal energy, the laws of attraction or in karma doesn't matter. What matters is whether you really believe in yourself and your ability. When I started in the wedding industry, it was a leap of faith. My friend called to say that he had bought a franchise of a wedding magazine, and he wanted me to come and sell for him. The position was as an independent contractor, commission-only, no salary, no base, and no draw against commissions. If I made a sale, I got paid. If I didn't, I got nothing. That, in itself, requires a belief in oneself. To complicate the decision, we had a 3-year old and one on the way. I had to give up the security of a steady job and paycheck, so I could go out on the road - every day - and sell advertising in our wedding magazine.

That pressure required a leap of faith; but, I was confident in my skill as a salesperson. I have never worried about providing for my family. There have been good times, and bad, but we've always had a roof over our heads and food on the table. How confident are you in your skills? I'm fortunate that my skill is in sales, but I have to have skills in the services I provide, to back that up. Yours might be the opposite. Your skill, and passion, may be in photography, or culinary arts, or transportation, officiating, or something else. You need to back those skills up with business skills, so you can get to follow your passion.

## Vision test

As you look back at your dots, can you also see the ones you skipped? Can you see the opportunities you passed on, or the ones you see now, that you didn't see at the time? Did you pass on an opportunity because, at the time, you thought it was too expensive or involved too much risk? Do you now see that you missed out on the possible return, because you didn't make the investment? Reflecting on those opportunities taken, and skipped, can give you a clearer vision to see the next opportunity. What opportunities are around you, right now? Which ones have you passed on, that you might just want to look at again? Take a look behind you for clarity. Then look forward, because we can't change the past, but we can change how we look towards our future. Who knows, you just might get lucky!

⌢

# WHAT ARE YOU WAITING FOR?

Before I get started, I want this to be a positive message for you. That said, what prompted this topic was the passing, too young, of a few industry and personal friends. It got me thinking about what, if anything, they wished they had done, either personally or professionally. There's no shortage of things to eat up our time: email, social media, family obligations, etc. Are you making time for the other things? Are you doing the things that give you the most pleasure, or that will have the greatest impact on your clients (which, hopefully, also gives you pleasure)?

I've written before about how you have the time for anything you prioritize, so I'm not going to rehash that here. Rather, I want you to reflect on what those things are. What is it that you've been delaying? What is it that you daydream about, but never take any steps towards accomplishing? You can't reach a target that you can't see. Yes, the journey is as important as the destination, but the destination gives you focus.

## Personal endeavors

What do you do when you're not working? I know that some of you are laughing now, because you're always working. Let me rephrase that. What would you like to be doing, if you weren't working all the time? Is it reading more books, or making quilts? Is it learning a new skill, or doing martial arts? Is it learning a new language or volunteering more? Whether it's a new skill, or one that has been gathering dust, what's stopping you from doing more of that now?

## You know what I was thinking?

My wife and I have a code phrase: *"You know what I was thinking?"*, which means that we're taking a trip to Home Depot! She dreams up a project for our house, and I have to build, rework, fix or create it. Some people call this the "Honey-Do" list, as in *"Honey, I need you to do this."* Some people dread this. I look forward to it, because I love working with my hands and I love fixing things. It gives me an excuse to dig into my tools and make some sawdust. Most of our projects aren't fixing anything, rather they're creating or re-doing something that's perfectly fine. We just love the process and the end result.

The thing is, I need that *"You know what I was thinking?"* to push me to get out the tools. Why? I love working with tools. So, why wouldn't I just get out to the garage without the question? It's just not a priority. My wife's asking the question changes my priorities at that time. I could resist, but I'm happily married (cue the smiley face), and I want to stay that way.

## Professional endeavors

What's your next big move at work? What have you been thinking about, but you just haven't gotten started? Have you been thinking about raising your rates? You have thought about adding a new product or service? Have you thought about attending a conference or networking event, but it never makes it on to your calendar? Once again, it's about priorities. In this digital world it's easy to get disconnected from your network. Yes, we make relationships, and even sales, through email and other digital platforms. But, deeper connections are made in person. We refer people we know, like and trust (again, credit to Bob Burg for that). People will know you, get to like you and trust you when you've had a more meaningful connection. Take that digital connection and strengthen it at a local networking event. Better yet, volunteer for that networking group, and show people that you're a giver, not a taker. People are more likely to refer you through your actions, over your words.

## Learning has never been easier

There's no shortage of learning opportunities these days. Between classes, workshops, conferences and online content, improving or picking up a new skill is easy... once you prioritize it. I listen to audio books while I'm driving. Instead of listening to the news, or music, I'm "reading" a book. Some are directly related to my work, and some are just interesting. I love when I'm reading a book that isn't directly related to my work, and I get ideas that I can apply to my business, and to yours.

## Getting new ideas when you least expect it

While I've done a lot of my learning by myself (learning Spanish and reading/listening to books), I love going to live events. It's what happens in the hallway, at the meals and at the bar where I've gotten some of my best ideas, where I've shared many ideas, and met some great people. Someone asks a question and the others in the group benefit. Or, you hear something that someone else is doing, and you think about how you can apply that to your business. Or, you hear something that someone else is doing and decide that it's not right for your business.

## You've got to be in it, to win it

The key is that you have to be there, to benefit. That's why it drives me crazy that the attendance at live events, whether local, regional or national, isn't higher. I prioritize my speaker training. I have the National Speakers Association conference dates blocked off years into the future. I usually don't even look at the schedule until I'm on the plane to the conference. I know that I'm going to meet new people, learn new things and come up with new ideas, regardless of who's speaking. Don't get me wrong, I will hear some great speakers. I trust the conference to ensure that. But, I also know that I'm going to learn as much, or more, in-between sessions. Some of my strongest relationships, both in the speaking industry, as well as the wedding/events industry, got their start in-between sessions at a conference.

Think back to the people you've met, the ideas you've gained and the inspiration that was sparked at a live event. If you've never attended an industry event, then ask your friends. Return on investment (ROI) isn't always about direct sales or dollars. It's also about relationships and connections that can and will help you in many ways. Yes, sometimes it's about getting referrals. Other times it's about having someone you can call, or message, with a question. Someone you can bounce ideas off. Just remember to be a giver, not a taker, and others will be more willing to give back to you.

Now what are you going to do? What small step can you take today that will get you closer to a personal or professional goal? What ideas are bouncing around in your head, but they never get out? It's been said that if you always do, what you've always done, you'll always get, what you've always gotten. If that acceptable to you, then keep on keeping on. If not, then do something different, or take a new small step today. I look forward to seeing you at an industry event and hearing your success stories.

# WHAT CROSSWORD PUZZLES CAN
# TEACH US ABOUT LIFE AND BUSINESS

Crossword puzzles are my diversion. I do one almost every day. It's both a brain stimulant and meditation for me. When I'm doing a puzzle my mind is focused, not wandering or multi-tasking. What's your diversion? For some of you it's Sudoku, or maybe a game on your phone or tablet. For others it may be yoga, or reading a book.

As my family and I live in the New York area, I get *The New York Times* delivered daily. I rarely get to read more than a few articles in a day, while eating breakfast, and I can get the same news on my NYTimes iPhone app. I get news alerts on my phone, so I'm up to date on the latest in world happenings. I find that reading the actual newspaper, as with reading a physical book, is a different experience than reading on a screen.

## Involve More Senses

When it comes to crossword puzzles, I like doing a physical puzzle versus using an app. I can do the same *New York Times* puzzle, the same day, on their app. I've tried it and I get too easily bored and distracted. It's too easy to flip between the puzzle and email or social media. That's why I like the analog version (pen and paper).

Even my millennial-age son now does the crossword puzzle on paper. He gets *The Wall St. Journal* delivered, so we have both puzzles to do. Our daily ritual is to make copies of each of the puzzles, so we can each do both of them (and don't worry - we always recycle them when we're finished).

## WordPlay

A few years ago, I watched a documentary called *Wordplay*, which is about *The New York Times* crossword, and the people who make the puzzles, edit them and solve them. You can probably find it on Netflix or a similar service. One thing I learned from watching it, was that Monday is the easiest day for *The New York Times* puzzle, and - as it turns out - also for *The Wall St. Journal*. The puzzle gets progressively more difficult each day through Saturday (which is the most difficult). I always thought Sunday was the hardest. The Sunday puzzle, while bigger, is the equivalent difficulty of a Thursday puzzle.

Bolstered by this knowledge, I started doing the Monday puzzles, in pen (with a tube of *Wite-Out* close by). Once I was able to finish the Monday puzzles, I started trying Tuesday. When I was able to finish the Tuesday puzzles pretty regularly, I went on the Wednesday, and so forth.

## A fresh set of eyes

Often, I'd have to walk away from a puzzle, and come back to it. Answers, that had previously eluded me, were suddenly clear. The puzzles towards the end of the week are particularly challenging. While the answers are often familiar, the clues become more obscure. There are times when I want to just give up and toss the puzzle in the recycling bin. After all, what's the loss? It's just a crossword puzzle, and no one will know - except me.

## It's just like life

And that's when it hit me... crossword puzzles are just like life and business. Some days the answers are obvious and easy, and some days the answers elude us. Some days we want to throw in the towel and call it quits, and others let us revel in our accomplishments. So, what's the difference? If I can come back and solve a puzzle that eluded me, why couldn't I solve it the first time? After all, I must have already had the knowledge and skills to get to the answer, so why didn't they work for me the first time?

## Some days are going to be more challenging

When I first tried solving the Friday and Saturday puzzles, it was very humbling. I would get a handful of the answers, at most. Looking at all of those unfilled boxes was depressing; but, something told me to keep trying. What I discovered was that there were always some answers that I could get, so I would just work my way out from those. In the movie *WordPlay*, they filmed different people (actors, ex-Presidents, and other notables) doing the same puzzle. They talked about how some people have to go in order, doing all of the Across clues in order, before doing the Down clues. While others went more randomly, working off a completed answer, going across and down, until they couldn't go any further.

## Structure or random?

Isn't that just like life? Some people have to go in order, and others go more unstructured. They may come to the same conclusion, they just get there in different ways. The other thing that's just like life, is that some people walk away, while others stick to it. Which are you? Do you walk away when things get tough? Do you come back and give it another shot, or toss it in the metaphorical recycle bin of life? In my book: "*Your Attitude for Success,*" I say that the difference between those who succeed, and those who don't, isn't ideas or money, it's action.

## Action, action, we want action

Ideas don't get you anything, unless you act on them; and, it's not just acting on your ideas, it's sticking to it. If it was easy, someone would probably already be doing it. And yes, sometimes we need to walk away, and come back with a clear head. Often, we need to get out of the environment to clear our heads. Have you ever come up with the elusive answer in the shower, or at your kid's soccer game? I'm sure there's a good psychological reason for this, but for the purposes of this article, let's just accept that it's happened to all of us before and it will happen again. Sometimes we just need to keep our eyes open, and sometimes we need to stop thinking about it for a while, and then come back.

The answers aren't always where we're looking. Artists and product designers get their inspiration from everywhere. The answers you seek may very well come from outside your industry. You have to be willing to look for them, and ready to adapt them to your needs. As I mentioned in another chapter, we have a phrase in the National Speakers Association: *"Adapt, don't adopt."* It means don't take someone else's idea, adapt it and make it your own.

## Be an original, not a copy

Too many people in our industry are trying to copy a competitor's ideas, instead of adapting what they see, and coming up with their own ideas. It's hard to copy someone else, because you're living their reality, not yours. You're actually copying their history. What you're seeing is their past ideas, brought to fruition. You don't know what new ideas they're working on. By the time you copy what you're seeing now, they may very well have something newer. So, are you an original or a copy? Do you give up, or do you stick to it and see your ideas through - especially when the going gets tough? The next big idea is waiting for you, don't give up.

## Thoughts and Ideas

# You can't change
# someone's mind

I'm right and you're wrong! That attitude is a recipe for disaster in business and in life. If you want to keep your significant-other happy, telling them that they're wrong is, let's just say, not a good plan. Similarly, if you want to keep your customers, and employees, happy, telling them they're wrong is counter-productive. The fact is that you can't change anyone else's mind. It's not yours to change, it's theirs. What you can do is provide them with information they didn't have, and then they may decide to come to a different conclusion.

How and when you provide them with that information is more of an art than a science. Every political ad is trying to provide us with information either about their candidate, or their opponent, to get us to change our minds. Which is more effective on you? The positive information, or the negative? While I would rather hear what you can do for me, instead of why the other business, or candidate is bad, those negative comments do have an effect.

## Please ignore that statement

My wife watches a lot of crime dramas on TV, which means I watch crime dramas on TV (did I mention that I'm happily married?). Many of you can picture the courtroom scene where a prosecuting attorney says something, the defense attorney objects, the judge allows the objection ("sustained") and then she instructs the jury to disregard what they just heard. That's impossible. You can't un-hear something. Now it's up to the defense attorney to provide information that will get the jury to change their minds about what they've just heard.

When we hear conflicting information, we consider the sources and decide which is more believable, trustworthy and/or influential. We also look to the amount or strength of the infor-mation. Let's say you were looking for a restaurant while on vaca-tion. You go to your favorite source (Yelp, TripAdvisor, Google, OpenTable...) and do a search. One restaurant comes up at the top of the search, but it's a "sponsored" listing, meaning they paid to be there. Do you assume them to be the best? Probably not with-out some corroborating evidence. In other words, did they also come up in organic results, or do they have a lot of reviews and a good rating. When it comes to reviews there are three things that matter: 1) the number of reviews 2) the average rating/score and 3) the recency.

## Who's right?

I travel extensively, so I also eat out a lot. When I'm searching for a restaurant I'll do a search for something in the area, maybe put in a few filters if I/we prefer a particular style, and see what comes up. Knowing that it takes a lot for me to give a 5-star rating to a res-taurant, I'm fine with looking at 4's and 3.5's. If there aren't a lot of choices in that range, I'll work my way down. But I also look at the number of reviews, as I know that with few total reviews, one low rating can bring the average down. I'll read the low rated review to see what that person, or those people had to say. If it's just a total rant, I'll usually ignore it. But if it's articulate, and specific in their critique, it will influence my decision.

## How's the Mac n' Cheese?

I was driving with my family in Florida and we passed a Bar-B-Que place. My sister and brother-in-law, who live in the area, hadn't seen this place before, and they love BBQ. So, I looked it up on Yelp and TripAdvisor to see the reviews. After reading a few reviews we started to get a picture of the food and service. The ribs were a universal favorite, with every review having very positive and emotional comments. The Mac n' Cheese was hit or miss, mostly miss. The more reviews we read, the more we wanted their ribs, but not their Mac n' Cheese. Then I came across someone who loved the Mac n' Cheese. Huh? Every other review that had mentioned it had a complaint (not enough cheese, too chewy, no flavor, etc.).

How could it be that this one person was in opposition to all of the other comments? Maybe she liked hers with only a little cheese, or under-cooked. Maybe it was her past experience with Mac n' Cheese – it's just like her mother made for her when she was a little girl. Did it change our minds about the Mac n' Cheese? If we went to this restaurant were we likely to order the Mac n' Cheese? No. The scales were already tipped against that. The only things that would have possibly changed our minds is if all of the negative Mac n' Cheese reviews were old, and the positive one(s) were more recent, or if recent reviews talked about how they didn't used to like it, but now they have a new Mac n' Cheese recipe, or chef, and now it's great.

## When you don't know, what you don't know

It's the same when your prospects are looking for someone in your category. It's not just THAT you have a lot of great reviews, it's WHAT those reviews say. What are the adjectives that they're using when they rave about you? What are they saying about your competitors? Reviewing a wedding isn't the same as reviewing a restaurant, but the psychology is similar. Potential customers are reading and are influenced by the specific words and phrases that your past customers are using in their reviews. If those words and phrases resonate with them, they'll be more likely to contact you. If they don't, they'll move on (and you may never know they were interested in the first place).

### How can you change their minds?

As I said in the beginning, you can't actually change the mind of your prospects. You can only provide them with information they didn't have, and they can choose to come to a different conclusion. First you have to have their attention, which is fleeting. Then you have to present that information in a way that is easy to consume. Many of you have heard me say that your brand is defined by the words of your past customers. Your reviews and testimonials are your brand. And many of you are using reviews and testimonials on your websites and in your marketing. Are you putting them where you have their attention? Are you making them easy to consume?

### Is anybody listening?

If you're putting them on a testimonials page on your website, check your analytics report to see if anyone is actually going there. In my consulting I have never seen a testimonial/reviews/kudos page that has a significant amount of traffic. Most are 1% to 2% of that site's total traffic, with many being well under 1%. That makes sense since we all know that you only put the best comments there, so why should we leave the page we're on to go see your Love-fest? Some of you have them on your sites, but down low on the page. How often do you get to the bottom of a web page these days? Not that often, and neither do your site's visitors. You need to put them where they're already looking, where you already have their attention, high up on the most popular pages.

And then you have to make them easy to consume by making them very short. The longer they are, the less likely they'll be read. I like to use the metaphor of a speed-bump in the road. It's one line and it makes you slow down to continue down that road. If you use one-line review snippets throughout the page, supporting your other site copy, it will slow your readers down, but not stop them. We want them to continue down the page as we influence them that they're in the right place and get them to take the action that we make clear (email, fill out your contact form, text, chat, etc.). You're not going to get them to pick up a phone and call you just because you want them to. They're on a web page, they're much more likely to take a digital next step (email, text, chat, contact form) than change to a phone call. They're the customer and they're driving this process, for now. They're only one click of their BACK button away from one of your competitors. Give them a reason to stay. Then give them a reason to move forward and contact you. But don't try to change their minds, it's not yours to change.

## Thoughts and Ideas

# From the Author

W ho is Alan Berg? If I had to answer this in one sentence, I'd say "I'm a Suburban Renaissance Man". I'm a husband, father, son, brother, friend, speaker, author, salesman, marketer, musician, handyman, consultant, teacher and, I've been told, an all-around nice guy. I'm passionate about my family and my work. I love being creative and working with my hands as well as my mind. That's one of the reasons there's a wrench in my personal logo.

I've worked in sales, marketing and sales management for over 25 years, over 20 in wedding media. I spent 11 years at The Knot (at the time the largest, busiest wedding media site in the world), most as Vice President of Sales and Vice President of The Knot Market Intelligence. I'm a professional speaker and proud member of the National Speakers Association, the leading organization for professional speakers, where I've been honored to earn my Certified Speaking Professional® (CSP), the highest earned designation for a professional member - which makes me one of only about 800 in the world. I'm also been privileged to be, as of this writing, one of only 33 Global Speaking Fellows in the world (through the Global Speakers Federation).

I revel in the success of others and truly believe that your success will lead to more success for me and for everyone. I believe that when you give first you'll get more than you could have ever asked for in return. I also believe in living for today, while planning for tomorrow. I know that this information can help you, as it has for so many others, and I appreciate you picking up my book. I look forward to hearing how you've implemented these ideas.

Thank you.

Please post your thoughts about this book on Amazon at: **www.ReviewMyBooks.net**

In addition to writing books and articles I have the privilege of traveling around the country, and internationally, performing keynote addresses and workshops in 14 countries, as well as doing in-house trainings. If you'd like to have me speak for your company, conference, group or association, train your sales and customer support teams or to have me review your website or help you with consulting or coaching services, please contact me directly:

email: **Alan@AlanBerg.com**

visit: **www.AlanBerg.com**

call/text: **732.422.6362**

international: **+1 732 422 6362**

WhatsApp: **+1.732.289.4842**

# ABOUT THE AUTHOR

Alan Berg is fluent in the language of business. He's been in marketing, sales and sales management for over 20 years, working with businesses, like yours, in the wedding and event industry. Before striking out on his own as a business consultant, author and professional speaker, he served as Vice President of Sales and The Knot Market Intelligence at The Knot (now The Knot World Wide), the time the leading life stage media company. In additional to his speaking and consulting he also serves as a consultant and Educator for WeddingWire, the leading wedding technology company, doing webinars, live presentations, writing articles and more. Alan is the wedding & event industry's only Certified Speaking Professional', the highest earned designation for a professional member of the National Speakers Association. And, as of this writing, he's one of only 33 Global Speaking Fellows in the world.

He's able to help new businesses and solopreneurs, as well as established players and corporations, understand and achieve their goals. Alan understands business as he's owned several of his own, including publishing two wedding magazines. He understands what it's like to make payroll, do the books, do collections, apply for a loan and manage/hire/fire/train employees. He knows what you're going through, feels your pain and can help ease it. Increasing sales and profitability are wonderful remedies!

Through his extensive experience, speaking and consulting domestically and internationally (14 countries, on 5 continents, and counting), Alan understands that the needs of wedding businesses are not that different from the needs of all businesses. You all want to find, capture and retain customers. If you're reading this book you want actionable content, not exhaustive homework and that's what you'll get. This book is designed to be read chapter by chapter, not necessarily front to back, so you can get to the action you need, faster. Get started now on your journey to greater success.

## Share Alan's unique inspirational, actionable content

If you'd like to have Alan speak for your company, conference, group or association, to thank your key partners for their referrals, for bulk copies of this book to inspire your team or members - including custom editions with your branding, and to find out about his website review and consulting services for your business, large or small (yes, even if you're the only employee), contact Alan directly:

email: **Alan@AlanBerg.com**

visit: **www.AlanBerg.com**

call/text: **732.422.6362**

international: **+1 732 422 6362**

WhatsApp: **+1.732.289.4842**

# WHAT PEOPLE ARE SAYING ABOUT ALAN'S SPEAKING AND SALES TRAINING

"My team and I attended a Mastermind with Alan Berg a few weeks ago and we LOVED it! Alan gave us some great insight on the wedding industry and tips and tricks we have already put into place."

Ian Ramirez,
Madera Estates, Conroe, TX

❧

"I think one of the main differences in your training is that our team left that day with strategies that they can immediately implement."

Steve Sanchez,
The JDK Group, Camp Hill, PA

❧

"I'd say the thing that is different about your training over others would be the practical application. I liked how we could stop you at any point and ask specific questions about obstacles we have faced."

Cory Gosik,
Sensational Host Catering,
North Maple Shade, NJ

❧

**"I believe Alan genuinely cares about my success.** It's like he has adopted me and my colleagues into his own family! **He is approachable, accessible, smart, funny and down to earth.** We love Alan!"

Justin Johnson,
Complete Weddings, Albuquerque, NM

❧

**"Alan is a fun and engaging presenter and his topics are relevant and on-trend. In a sea full of 5,500 people, Alan stood out."**

Sarah Alexander,
The Celebrant Society, Sydney, Australia

❧

**"Fantastic! Seriously. Don't know how he takes a topic like reviews and actually makes it engaging, but he does!"**

Jan Oelke,
Relics Vintage Rentals, Milwaukee, WI

❧

**"If you want to just hear how wonderful you and your company is, call your mother. If you want to make your business grow and convert for you, call Alan."**

David Rothstein,
DRS Music, Chicago, IL

❧

If you'd like to find out how Alan can help you, and your sales team (whether you're a team of 1 or 50) through speaking for your group or association, a website review, or private sales training at your location, anywhere in the world, call/text/email:

email: **Alan@AlanBerg.com**

visit: **www.AlanBerg.com**

call/text: **732.422.6362**

international: **+1 732 422 6362**

WhatsApp: **+1.732.289.4842**

or visit **www.AlanBerg.com**

# HOW TO MARKET AND SELL YOUR BOOK

A Guide for Beginners

**Makonnen Sankofa**

Published in London, England by
Independent Publishing Network in 2022.

**ISBN:** 9781803520667

**Editor**
Jessie Raymond

**Cover Designer**
Muhammad Arslan

# CONTENTS

# YOUR BOOK, YOUR RESPONSIBILITY

When it comes to the success of your book, one of the most critical factors is marketing. A common mistake many authors make, is that they write a book and think they have done all the work. You can write an excellent book, but if it's not marketed properly, it's likely that you will experience low book sales and you will struggle to raise awareness of your book. When marketing your book, you need to put in as much dedication as you did when writing the book, especially if you're a self-published author and you don't have the backing of a traditional publisher, a marketing team, or a marketing manager.

Many self-published authors make the mistake of expecting their publisher to market their book for them. In reality, unless you have a written agreement with them, it's not the publisher's responsibility to market your book. It's different if your book has been traditionally published because traditional publishers do a lot to help market books for authors, and they have big networks and strong connections with bookstores and media outlets, which makes them very useful when it comes to marketing a book. However, many writers are self-published authors who have either published the book directly themselves or used an independent publisher to assist them with self-publishing their book. If that's the case, you must read very carefully what's in the agreement with your publisher. If there is no mention of marketing services being included, then don't expect them to market your book.

A publisher's job is to publish your book. However, there are some publishers who offer marketing services as well as publishing. In this case, know exactly what marketing services you have paid for, and only expect the publisher to deliver on the marketing services covered in the agreement you have with them. For example, if your agreement with a publisher is for them to publish your book and host two speaking engagements during the year for you to promote your book to an audience, know that that's what you should be getting and don't expect more marketing than that from the publisher. If there wasn't marketing services included in the agreement with your publisher, don't hold your publisher accountable for not marketing your book. You may have publishers who give you additional promotion that wasn't even included in your agreement. But don't expect that from them because it's not the publisher's responsibility to market your book. It's your book, so take charge of marketing it.

You may want your book traditionally published, so you have more support with marketing and selling your book. Traditional publishers prefer to publish books for people who already have a big following (e.g., a famous person, an influencer, or someone with a lot of followers on social media). If you have already published your book, traditional publishers won't take you on unless you're re-publishing your book as a new book or publishing another book.

One of the benefits of having your book traditionally published, is that a traditional publisher can give your book a lot of exposure and they can get your book put in places that you may not be able to as a self-published author. Another one of the benefits of having your book traditionally published, is that a traditional publisher will pay you a lump sum of money in advance before your book is even available for sale in stores. A traditional publisher will usually pay a first-time author an advance between £3,000 and £9,000 for the rights to their book.

Self-published authors make up to 70% royalties from sales of their books. Traditionally published authors don't get paid royalties until the traditional publisher has made back the lump sum given to authors in advance. After that, most traditionally published authors are paid 10% royalties. With some traditional publishers, if your book doesn't make enough sales to cover the advance they paid you, then you will be required to pay back the difference between your sales and the money they gave you. You may also be expected to pay the cost of posting the books back to you, which can be very expensive, especially if the books are being shipped from another country.

A disadvantage of trying to go the traditional publisher route, is that it can be very time-consuming, and there is no guarantee in the end that a traditional publisher will decide to publish your book. For example, you could be contacting traditional publishers for a year or more, without being offered a publishing contract. Another disadvantage of having your book traditionally published, is that you give away creative control of your book. This is because traditional publishers can make you change parts of your book that you may want to keep.

Even if you get your book traditionally published, you should still do your best to market your book. Use the internet to search for retailers who you can sell wholesale copies of your book to. You can use search engines like Google or Yahoo to browse bookshops by entering key words that match what you're looking for. You can also find information about bookstores on social media websites such as Facebook, Instagram, and Twitter. Look for sellers worldwide and create a list of their contact details. Message your potential book sellers to let them know that you would like them to sell your book. Or, send a message asking your potential book sellers about the procedure of getting your book sold by them.

When you message them, you could include the following information about your book: an overview, a brief summary of the different chapters, what makes your book unique from other books that have been written on the same subject, the target market, the wholesale price, and the suggested retail price. Create a Microsoft Word document or PDF which has all that information as a template. Based on the person you're messaging; you may choose to add or remove some of the wording in the template text.

You can also visit local bookshops in-person and request that they stock copies of your book. It's generally easier to get your book stocked in local independent bookshops and independent retailers (especially in physical locations) in comparison to getting your book stocked in more established retail shops that are part of a big chain of shops. The reason for this, is because you can go into a local shop and meet the person that owns or manages the business, who is able to make a decision there and then about whether to stock your book in their shop.

But if you go into a more established bookshop or retailer which is owned by a big company, it's less likely that someone in the shop has the power to make the decision about whether your book can be stocked there. With most big companies, there is usually a strict procedure which those shops follow in order to determine which books they stock in their shops. You can ask staff at those shops about the procedure you must follow in order to get your book stocked there. Or, you can go online and visit the company's website to see if they have information about how to get your book stocked in their shop. If there is no information about this on the company's website, then you can contact them by the email or phone number that has been provided on the company's website.

# PRE-RELEASE MARKETING AND SALES

Pre-launch promotions of your book will help to raise awareness of the product. As an author, you want to get as much exposure of your book as possible. Having a good pre-launch will help you build momentum going into the release date of your book. Think about when a new smartphone is being released. If the latest iPhone or Samsung smartphone came out but nobody knew about it until the day the product was released, the product launch wouldn't be as effective. Marketing a book before its release, makes people aware of the launch date. Whilst people anticipate the launch of your book, they can plan ahead and save money to buy your book when it is released.

Create interest and excitement around your book before its release. Start posting info about your book on social media and talk to people about your upcoming book. When you are doing interviews and other speaking engagements, mention that you have an upcoming book coming out soon. Something you could do, is give the customer a sample of your book by sharing with them either a chapter from your book or a few poems from your book. The reason you give out a sample of content from your book, is to get someone to read or listen to the sample, so that they will be tempted to purchase the book. Another thing you could do, is a giveaway competition where the winner gets a free copy of your book as a prize. Giveaway competitions are a great way to collect data from people, such as email addresses and phone numbers. The aim of the giveaway, is to get leads that you can follow up on, with the goal of converting those leads into sales.

You may wonder why someone would want to pre-order your book when they can purchase your book when it is released. As an incentive to get people to pre-order your book, you may decide to sell pre-orders of your book at a discounted price. The benefit of putting books on pre-order, is that you receive payment in advance from your customers. The more book sales you make via pre-order, the closer you are to breaking-even on the cost of publishing your book.

There are a variety of ways that you can take pre-orders of your book (these methods also apply to taking orders in general):

## Cash or Card

You can take payments from customers in-person via cash or card (provided you have a card reader machine). I recommend SumUp Air Card Reader, which is available in USA and most European countries. There is a small one-off fee to purchase the device. There are no monthly costs; you are charged a fee of 1.69% per transaction. SumUp works by pairing the card reader to your smart mobile device (such as phone or tablet). You need to download the SumUp App from the Google Play Store or Apple Store and then complete the necessary set up steps through the app. To start taking payments, pair up your device to your phone using Bluetooth. The SumUp Air Card Reader accepts contactless and chip and payments.

## Payment Link

Send a payment link to your customers. This will be a website link to a financial services company (e.g., Stripe or PayPal) that accepts payment from customers online. First, you will need to create an account with whatever company you chose to use to accept payments from your customers. Then, you will need to create a payment link to send to customers who wish to purchase your book.

If your using Stripe, you can customise the product checkout page to show your book's name, the price of your book, and an image of your book. You can also customise the checkout page so you can collect details of your customer such as their name, postal address, phone number, and email address. It is important you have that information for delivering the book to your customer. The benefit of using Stripe, is that the checkout process is simple. Customers don't need to set up an account or log into their account to send money to you. Instead, they just go on the product checkout page from the link you send them and make a one-time payment. It can take the customer less than one minute to make a payment via Stripe.

## Bank Transfer

This payment method would be most suitable when receiving money from someone with a bank account in the same country as your bank. Otherwise, high bank charges will apply by doing international bank transfers. It probably won't be a viable option to take orders of your book via international bank transfers because the fees the customers have to pay to do a bank transfer could be even higher than the cost of your book. Even if the bank fees are less than the cost of your book, there still is cheaper ways customers can send money to you from abroad.

## International Money Transfer

You may decide to use international money transfer companies such as Western Union, Sendwave, WorldRemit, or MoneyGram. You wouldn't necessarily use those companies with domestic money transfers (if you live in Western countries). It is most likely you would use those payment methods in situations when you're taking an international payment from someone abroad (in Africa, Asia, the Caribbean) and your customer is more familiar with using one of those payment methods, or the customer can't use another alternative payment method. For example, the customer may be in a country where he/she can't set up a PayPal account from within that country.

## Your Website

If you have your own website, you may want to direct customers to make pre-orders of your book directly from your website. You should use a secure payment processor such as Visa Checkout, WorldPay, or PayPal. This will protect the customers details from fraud and give the customer confidence buying from your website

## Amazon KDP

If you are anticipating selling physical copies of your book internationally, you may want to check to see what countries your book can be shipped to via Amazon KDP. If Amazon KDP doesn't deliver physical book copies to people in a particular country, you may be able to sell your book in Kindle (eBook) format to people in those countries, providing they have an Amazon account. When uploading your Kindle (eBook) to be published, there is an option you can select which will allow you to take pre-orders from customers who choose to buy your book in Kindle (eBook).

# BOOK LAUNCH AND ONLINE EVENTS

When it comes to book launches, you can have multiple book launches. You can have a physical or online book launch. You can launch your book in different countries or cities. If you want, you can have both a physical and an online book launch. Having book launches in different locations will raise awareness of your book to a larger audience. Online book launches are likely to be more cost-effective, but in-person book launches offer a more personal touch because the author and the audience will see each other face-to-face and they can interact with each other.

If you're having a physical book launch, I would suggest considering featuring your book launch at an event that is already scheduled. That way, you don't have to worry about the cost of hiring a building and the other costs that go into organising a book launch. The higher the costs associated with your book launch; the more sales you will need to break-even and make a profit from the event. There is no point of spending a lot of money on organising a book launch, if you know you're not going to break-even. Unless, the reason for your book launch is not for financial gain.

If you want to have a physical book launch, speak to people who own or manage businesses such as bookshops, restaurants, cafes, coffee shops, pubs, and bars. Try to make a deal with one of those businesses to host your book launch at their venue for free, in exchange for you bringing potential customers to their venue that may patronise their business. If you're a member of a church and your able to get free access to host your book launch at the church building; consider hosting your book launch there, especially if your book has a theme based on the same religious views of the church you attend.

Hosting an online book launch is great because it's cheap and you can reach a global audience. You can always have a book launch across multiple platforms online. For example, you could have a book launch on Zoom, on Instagram, and on Clubhouse. If you're going to have an online book launch or an online event surrounding your book, create a form or questionnaire to collect data from registrants.

After the event, you can follow up on those registrants by sending them an email with information about your book and the link to where your book can be purchased. Sending out follow up emails, is a great way of reminding people about purchasing your book. You may even have some people who registered for the event but didn't attend the event; those people may buy your book when they receive that email. Follow up emails are important because they can help you to maximise your book sales.

Collecting email addresses is very useful because you can add those email addresses to your mailing list, so you can email those people when you're sending out further information about your book or when you're appearing at an upcoming event. You can also send them information if you release a new book. There are platforms such as Eventbrite or Zoom, where you can create an online registration form for your event. Develop a campaign to constantly grow your email list, such as hosting free webinars or teleseminars and requiring attendees to register to access the event.

Online events allow you to not only reach an international audience but also attract people from different parts of the country who would not have travelled to your event if it was a physical one. In general, online events are much more cost-effective than physical events because you save money you would have had to spend on hiring a venue and on the cost of your transportation.

When you are speaking at online events, have a professional background theme that is relative to your book. On websites such as Zoom or Streamyard, you can customise your own background (provided that your PC or Mac meets the system requirements). Customising your display background with your book cover and/or branding of your book, is a good way to advertise your book. If you need someone to design your customised display background, I suggest going on fiverr.com and getting a freelancer to do the job for you. If you don't customise your screens display background with graphics, you could have a banner of your book in the background or you could put your book on display in the background. If you have written more than one book, you could have your other book/s visibly on display in the background (especially if you're also going to talk about your other book/s).

# YOUR BOOK IS A BUSINESS

As an author, you are more than just a writer. You are also a business owner selling a product. That is the mindset you must have to get the best results from selling your books. An effective way to increase not only book sales but also your book business, is to offer additional products and services that are relevant to the book you have written. For example, if you have written a book about fitness, sport, health, wellbeing, cooking, etc., then you could deliver courses or sessions which complement the book you have written.

If you design a new course based on content from inside your book; you could include a copy of your book for everyone who signs up for the course, or you could suggest that people who attend your course, buy your book. By doing a course, it will raise awareness of your book and it can lead to more book sales. People attending your course will benefit from getting your book because it's relevant to them as it will help them with the course you're teaching. Introducing your book to people through your course, is a great way to market and sell your book naturally.

You can build a brand around your book by selling additional merchandise such as bags, backpacks, t-shirts, mugs, stationery, etc. This can be very effective, especially with a children's book where you brand your merchandise based on the character/s from your book. You can either sell your book individually or as a bundle with your other items. Selling book bundles is a great way to increase profits. There are several websites that allow you to design customised products. Some of those online businesses, allow you to order your product to be shipped to the customer directly. A benefit of this, is that it keeps your costs down because you don't have to spend money in advance on buying bulk orders of stock. Another benefit, is that you don't have to store the stock at a physical location.

When you go to events, sell other items that complement your book. If you have written a book on health and wellbeing, you could sell some health supplements or herbal teas. If your book is about beauty, you could sell skincare products. If you're a chef and you have written a book about food, you could sell bottles of your own sauce. My book is about Rastafari. When I went to events selling my book; I sold other add-ons such as pendants, wristbands, CDs of my talks, clothing, and posters. The items I sold were relevant to my book because they were Rastafari themed.

A book should only be the beginning of your relationship with a reader/customer. Use your book as a key to open the door to other ways of generating income. Once someone has bought from you once, they will usually be comfortable buying from you again unless they had a bad experience with you the first time. You should try to get repeat business from your readers/customers. Think about what other products and services you can offer to your readers/customers that will benefit them and help to grow your business.

You can use your day-to-day occupation to promote your book (depending on your occupation) by starting a conversation with your colleagues and customers about your book. This strategy should work well, especially if you have a job where you have a lot of spare time to speak to your customers and/or colleagues. Those jobs would likely be (but not limited to) a hairdresser, a barber, a beautician, a fitness instructor, a taxi driver, or a teacher. With your regular customers and colleagues, you would have already created a relationship with them over time. So, you can bring up the topic of your book as a natural part of the conversation without it coming across as if you're just trying to randomly sell them something.

The more you talk about your book, the more confident you will become doing this and it will improve your conversational skills, which will help you when you're speaking to other people about your book in the future. Even if you have spoken to someone and haven't sold a copy of your book to that person at the time, you may have had a great conversation and that person may decide to purchase your book at a later date. If you have a positive interaction with someone, you should maintain a positive spirit and energy when speaking to the next person about your book. This is because the next person you speak to, may buy your book from you. Speaking about your book is like practicing a skill or exercising — the more you do it, the more confident and better you become at it.

When you have a conversation about your book, don't just think about selling your book. You should think about the value of your book and how it will benefit the person reading it. Speak passionately about why you have written the book and share your views about some of the content included in the book. If you encompass those things in your conversation and make it sound interesting, you will often get people who will tell you that they want to buy your book rather than you having to ask them for the sale. But be ready to close the sale if necessary because sometimes customers need a bit of a *nudge* to get them to buy a product.

When it comes to buying non-essential products such as luxury items, people buy from people. Therefore, you may find that some people will buy from you just to support you because they're buying into you rather than into the book. For someone who doesn't know you, you have to start from scratch by building a rapport with them. However, regular customers or people you already know are warm leads. But those warm leads won't necessarily buy your book. You will still need to get them interested in buying your book. Don't be discouraged if family, friends, or people you know don't buy your book.

If you have the right marketing strategies and sales techniques in place, you will sell your book to a higher volume of people. There are different angles to approach different people when selling your book. You can appeal to people based on the content and valuable information in your book; you can appeal to people emotionally through your personality.

Or, you can target your potential customers based on understanding their emotions.

You should sell your book in different formats because we live in a modern age where people have preferences as to what format they want a book in. There are some people who prefer the traditional physical copy of a book—in paperback or hard copy. There are others who prefer reading eBooks on their electronic devices. You also have some people who like listening to audiobooks instead of reading. You want to make your book as easily accessible to your audience as possible. By having your book in all formats, you maximise potential sales because some people won't buy your book unless it's in the format they desire.

Create an email mailing list. To do this, you will need to collect email addresses. If you decide to sell your books via your own website, have a landing page—a page you give away something for free and in return the customer must enter their name and email address to unlock the free reward. The aim of this, is to gather information from the individual so you can market your product to them. Once you've added someone to your mailing list, you send them emails to market your book. Those emails can include: brief info about your book, a link to where your book can be purchased, content taken from your YouTube channel, posts about important dates that link in with your book, or information about your speaking engagements relating to your book. When sending emails to people on your mailing list, make sure to send emails via blind carbon copy (BCC) or another way where it keeps other people's email addresses confidential.

# CLOSE THE SALE

There are several ways; directly or indirectly, that you can ask for or prompt the sale of your book. Your approach should be influenced by factors such as the environment you are in at the time, the person you are speaking to, and the way the conversation is going. The direct way is to literally ask someone if they would like to buy a copy of your book. Before you do this, add something of value to the conversation or message.

For example, if you are going to send a message on WhatsApp or Facebook; send a video clip of you speaking about your book. Give the person some time to watch the video. Later on, send them a follow up message. Ask them, "What do you think of the video?" If they like the video and respond positively, follow that up with a direct question: "Would you like to get a copy of my book?" or "Please support me and get a copy of my book." Many people are often too shy to ask directly for the sale, but those who don't ask, don't get. Remember, it's a numbers game to do with the law of averages and maximising book sales. As we already know, not everyone you ask is going to buy your book.

But the more people you ask to buy your book; the more people who will buy your book, especially if you have given them a good reason to do so.

When asking for the direct sale, you should be careful about the manner in which you try to close the sale. You want to ask or prompt someone to buy your book without coming across as desperate. Don't go straight for the sale when people don't know about the value of what they're buying. Try to close sales but don't be too pushy; you don't want to become seen as that friend or person people know, who is always trying to sell them something they don't want.

Another approach you can use to try to close sales, is to prompt people to buy your book in an indirect way. For example, you could post some information about your book and then state: "The book is available on Amazon." You haven't told them to buy your book directly but you have mentioned where the book is available to be purchased.

When you're writing information or text promoting your book, always make sure there is something of value in the message rather than just sending a link and asking someone to buy your book. You can add value to your message by providing a description of your book or by including something that you mentioned in your book in the message you send out. By doing this, you want to tempt people to find out more about your book. You can also tailor the message to suit the individual by adding their name and/or giving information in your book that you believe will interest them. This adds a personal touch to your message. It also lets people know that you are addressing them directly rather than making them think they have received a generic message which you sent to everyone on your marketing list.

When speaking to someone in-person, you should be able to gauge the level of interest someone has in your book by the way the interaction between you and them is going and also by the person's body language. There will be situations when someone gives you the *greenlight* for the sales close. This will come in the form of a hint. You can detect this hint by either; something the person says to you, the person's level of engagement when speaking to you about your book, and/or the person's body language. If someone is hinting to you that they are interested in your book, try to close the sale of the book before you allow them to walk away.

Nowadays, most people tend to use their bank card to make payments. Make sure when you're doing events in-person, you always have your card reader with you. This will minimise the possibility of you missing out on sales. If you take cash only payments, there is always the possibility that someone could run out of cash because they've spent all their money already. For example, you're at an event where someone wants to buy your book but they have already spent all of their money buying products from other stallholders at the event. If you don't have a card reader, you will lose out on that sale. And that same scenario can happen to you at an event on more than one occasion.

Some people may not buy from you on the spot, but they will take down details of where your book is available and they will buy your book later. However, some people will take down details from you about where your book can be purchased but forget to buy your book or lose interest in buying your book. Therefore, you need to seek and capitalise on impulse buyers. Ideally, you want people to buy you book from you on the spot because once they leave (especially at events), your chances of selling that book are slim because a person has so many other things on their mind and you no longer have control to influence the sale when you're not with them.

It's so important to build a rapport with the people you're talking to about your book. People buy books for different reasons. Many people like meeting authors in-person. Some people will buy your book because of the personal touch being that you're the author of the book, who is standing in front of them and interacting with them. There are people who will buy your book to support you or because they like you. You will have those who will buy your book because the topic interests them. And others will buy you book for a family member, relative, partner, or friend.

Mention to people that they can buy your book as a gift for someone. There will be times when you are speaking to a person who your book is not targeted at, but that person knows someone who your book is aimed at. For example, you have written a children's book and you're talking to an adult about your book. Although that person is over the age group of your book, he/she has a five-year-old son and a seven-year-old niece who your book would be suitable for.

Another example, you've written a book for women and you're speaking to a man. In this case, try to get the man to buy your book as a gift for either a female member of his family, his girlfriend, or a female friend he has. Sometimes people will buy gifts for more than one person.

Always be ready to ask questions to find out information from people because not everyone is going to mention to you that they know people who your book would suit. You have to be the one to get people to think about buying your book as a gift. You can encourage people to buy your book by using the indirect approach to prompt them. Below are template examples of the kind of statements you can make:

**"I think your daughter will love this as a gift."**

**"Go on, treat your girlfriend. She will be really happy with you that you have thought about her. You know how women always like getting gifts? She will appreciate it."**

**"I guarantee he/she will enjoy reading this book."**

**"If I was you, I would buy a book for both your children. You can't buy for one and not for the other, can you?"**

**"Your husband would benefit from reading this book. If I was you, I would get it for him."**

**"One of my friends bought this for his wife last week and she loves the book."**

When you leave your home to go out, keep copies of your book on you. If you are a woman, you can put a few copies of your book in your handbag. If you are a male, you can get a small shoulder bag and keep a few copies of your book in there. Or, you can put some books in your backpack that you take with you when you are travelling around. If you go gym or do sports, carry a few copies of your book in your gym bag or sports bag.

You never know who you may bump into or who you may speak to, so always be ready. (1) You could be going somewhere on public transport and you see someone you know who just happens to be on the same bus or train as you. (2) You could be going somewhere and you meet a friend who introduces you to someone. (3) You could be going to get your hair done and you get into a conversation with someone else who is also at the barbershop or hair salon. (4) You could meet someone new at a social event you go to.

All those situations mentioned in the last paragraph; can potentially lead to sales of your book if you have conversations with people about your book. When you go out and take your book with you; also take your card reader with you, so you can take card payment in case someone doesn't have any cash on them.

# MARKETING AND SELLING AT EVENTS

As an author, you should go to events and places where you can promote your book to make sales. These events and places include markets, book festivals, family fun days, fairs, exhibitions, pop-up shops, etc. The places and type of events to go to will vary from author to author because authors have different target markets. So, it's important that you decide to go to events and places where people from your target audience will be at. As an author, it is essential that you know who your target market is.

A common mistake many authors make, is that they don't have a target market and they try to sell their book to everyone. You will waste time, energy, and money doing this. You need to narrow down who you are aiming to sell your book to. You should have a primary target market and a secondary target market. Your primary target market is the main people you want to buy your book. Your secondary target market is made up of people who may also be interested in buying your book, but they're not your main target market.

To maximise exposure of your book and

to increase sales, you need to be proactive by finding events and places where you can sell and/or market your book. You should browse the internet to find events, speak to people to see if they know any upcoming events, check publications, and check activity in social media groups such as WhatsApp, Facebook, and Instagram. Do not wait to be contacted about speaking engagements; as that will limit your opportunities to showcase your book, because you may only be contacted now and again about speaking engagements. And even if you get contacted about a speaking engagement; it may not be a speaking engagement you want to do.

People often post in social media groups about different events that are taking place. Once you see an event you like, contact the organiser and enquire about featuring at that event. You can find events by doing a simple Google search. You can also browse events on Eventbrite. On Facebook, join author groups and other groups that are relevant to the topic of your book. Then, search for events in those groups. If you find an event you want to be part of, contact the organiser of the event. By going to events, you can network with other people and find out about other events happening in the future.

Some speaking engagements you will be paid, some you won't get paid, and some will require you to pay to speak. It all depends on the kind of event and the policy of the event that the organiser has in place. If you're doing a speaking engagement at a physical location, speak to the organiser about having a stall to sell your book there. If you're doing a speaking engagement online, always mention where your book is available and put the link to where your book can be purchased in the chat (where possible).

Speaking engagements are good because it can lead to more sales of your book. For example, there may be people in the audience who can relate to your speech so they decide to buy your book. Or, there could be people who found your talk interesting and they buy your book to get more information on the topic you have written about. If you're doing a physical speaking engagement, always carry copies of your book and take your chip and pin machine with you. You could even ask the organiser if you can have a table or designated area to sell you books from (speak to the organiser about this privately in advance).

If you are going to organise an event, do a collaboration with an organisation or other individuals. This is because it's likely you will get more exposure of your book from working with other people than you will from working by yourself. Also, organising an event by yourself means you will need to invest more time and money into marketing the event to get people to come. As an author, you want to focus on selling books without having a lot of other tasks to do. Another disadvantage of organising an event yourself; is that it can be expensive to hire a building, and you may need to sell a lot of books to cover the cost of renting the building. So, I recommend that you participate in events that are already scheduled to take place rather than organise an event for yourself (unless you have a big following).

Speaking at an event that you put on in collaboration with others or an event already taking place is good because you are in an environment where you will meet people you would never have come across if you had done the event on your own. Therefore, you have the opportunity to sell copies of your book to a wider audience which is beyond just the people within your network. There's no point in wasting your money by putting on an event to sell books to your family, relatives, and friends because you can sell or try to sell your book to those people anytime you want. If you want to be successful with selling copies of your book, you need to prioritise selling your book to people you don't always have access to.

Markets can be a good place for you to sell your book, especially if the theme of the market is relevant to your book and/or the kind of people at that market are your target audience. A reason why markets can be a good place to sell books, is because people go to markets looking for products to buy. Another benefit of doing speaking engagements and selling books at events, is that you have the opportunity to network. On several occasions, I have been to events selling my books and then been invited to do a radio show interview by someone I met at that event. Each time I have done one of those radio show interviews; it has led to sales of my book, increased awareness of my book, and/or led to another opportunity to promote my book.

Sometimes, it will take people several times to see your book or hear you talk about your book before they will commit to buying your book. That's why it's important to be consistent and stay in the spotlight by doing regular events and posting regular content about your book on social media. Selling and marketing your book takes time, effort, energy, and patience. Don't expect to get rich overnight from selling your book.

It's important to write a book on a topic you're really into because that way, you will sound more passionate when speaking about the content in your book. Regardless of whether you are speaking to a large audience or a small audience, you should enjoy talking about your book. A high number of people listening to you speak about your book; means there is good potential for sales, based on the volume of listeners. But it doesn't necessarily mean you will get a lot of book sales. You could deliver a speech to a large audience and sell only a few books. In contrast, you could deliver your speech to a smaller audience and sell a higher volume of books. So, remain positive whether you're speaking to a large or small audience. Approach smaller audiences as opportunities to connect closer with those people, which can lead to them becoming followers of your work.

There are various days in the year which are significant to different people for different reasons. You should book events and speaking engagements throughout the year to promote your book, especially for important dates that are celebrated throughout the year (which are relevant to the topic of your book). For example, if you have written a book on Black History, schedule a line-up of events during Black History Month. If you have written a book about mental health, schedule events during Mental Health Awareness Month. If you have written a book about womanhood, arrange to do a speech during an event on International Women's Day.

# SELLING YOUR BOOK ONLINE

It may be cost-effective to sell your books on other websites rather than on your own website. This is because the cost of designing your website or hosting fees can outweigh the money made from your book sales. There are many popular websites where you can sell your book without any hosting fees. These websites include Amazon via KDP, Waterstones, Barnes & Nobles, and Book Depository. If you already have an existing website; you could sell your book there, which saves you from spending money on having another website. If you are going to sell your books on your website, also sell your books on popular websites to increase your chances of maximising book sales.

It's more likely people will remember to buy your book if they can buy it on a popular website rather than your website, especially if it's someone you have meet at an event in-person. Many people shop on websites like Amazon, eBay, Waterstones, WH Smiths, Barnes & Noble, and Walmart. Those retailers are seen as credible because of their brand awareness. In general, people feel they are better protected from scams and fraud by buying their products from well-established companies rather than unknown websites run by individuals or small businesses. With websites such as Amazon and eBay, the buyer is comfortable because they know they can file a claim to get their money back if there is an issue with the order.

Amazon is the biggest and most popular online bookshop in the world. You can sell your book via Amazon KDP or via Amazon Seller Central (subject to the country you live in). When selling your book via Amazon KDP, you are only charged fees once the book sells. If you sell your book via Amazon Seller Central, you have to pay a monthly fee to Amazon and you will also have a commission from your sales deducted. With Amazon KDP, Amazon prints the book and delivers it to the customer.

If you sell your book through Amazon Seller Central, you have to either ship the book directly to the customer, or you can ship the book to Amazon and Amazon will ship the book to the customer. To sell a book using Amazon KDP, you need to login to your Amazon KDP account and upload your book on that platform. To sell via Amazon Seller Central, you just list your product for sale (no uploading of your book is needed). One of the main disadvantages of selling with Amazon KDP compared to Amazon Seller Central, is that it takes a long time to get paid with Amazon KDP. Amazon Seller Central pay within a minimum of five working days. However, Amazon KDP pays monthly royalties 60-90 days in arrears. Amazon Seller Central also pay higher commission than Amazon KDP.

There are several benefits of selling your book via Amazon KDP:

- Amazon KDP prints the book and ships the order to the customer, which saves you from having to spend time on fulfilling your order.

- No need to stock copies of your book to ship to Amazon customers. This is beneficial because it can help you manage your cash-flow as there is no need to spend money buying wholesale copies of your book in bulk.

- No need for storage space to keep stock copies of your book.

- Amazon KDP ship books worldwide.

- They don't charge international customers more money for shipping. The benefit of this, is that the advertised price of your listing doesn't need to go up. If you were shipping the book directly to the customer, your shipping costs would go up accordingly and you would need to pass that extra cost onto the customer, which means the price of buying your book becomes higher.

- If you go on holiday or move abroad; you can still sell copies of your book via Amazon KDP and they will fulfil your customer orders as normal, provided that Amazon shipping is available in the country where your book is being delivered to.

- They sometimes do promotions where they reduce the price of your book for customers and pay you the same royalties as if the book sold at full price.

- You have the option to choose expanded distribution, which means Amazon will sell your book through third-party companies and you will be paid for those sales.

- The process of purchasing is simplified. For one, it lists the different formats of your book on one page. Secondly, it only takes a single click to buy your book in Kindle (eBook) from once you're on the product page of the book.

Another popular website is eBay. Like Amazon, the advantages of selling on eBay include customer familiarity, trust, and the ease of transaction. A benefit of selling on eBay in comparison to Amazon KDP, is that eBay take less fees than Amazon. With eBay, you can be a seller with a subscription or a seller without a subscription. Sellers without a subscription will get 1,000 free listings a month, which lasts for five, seven or 10 days. If a seller wants to list more items or list items for one or three days, they will have to pay 35p an item. Sellers with a £19.99 monthly subscription will get 1,000 free standard listings a month, plus 100 shorter one or three-day listings.

If you are listing products on eBay or another website, you can order wholesale copies of your book through Amazon KDP and then sell the copies on eBay or another website at a retail price. With eBay, you receive payments from customers instantly. In contrast to Amazon KDP, where you are paid 60-90 days in arrears. But unlike Amazon KDP, people can't download eBooks or audiobooks via eBay. Other places where you can sell your book in eBook format include Barnes & Nobles, Waterstones, Ingram Spark, Blurb, Lulu, and Etsy. If you have enlisted your book with Kindle Unlimited, you will not be able to sell your eBook on any other platform while your book is still enrolled with Kindle Unlimited. People who have Kindle Unlimited subscriptions can read your eBook for free, and you are paid in royalties per page of your book that someone reads.

## Amazon Author Central

An Amazon Author Central account is an author's profile page on Amazon. It's free to have an Amazon Author Central account and it's useful because people can click on your profile on Amazon and find out more information about you and the different books you have written, all in one place. So, rather than having to send people different links to webpages of where your books are available, you just send them one link to where they can purchase your books from (if you have written more than one book).

The benefit of having all your books available to order from one place, is that it can help you maximise your sales. This is because a person could be about to purchase one of your books and then when then they see you have written another book, they may decide to buy the other book you have written as well. But if you send them a link to a webpage where only one of your books can be bought from; their less likely to purchase your other book because it's not in the same place as the original book the person came to buy.

## Amazon Adverts

You can pay for Amazon to do advertisements of your book on their website; this can be a placement where Amazon put your book at the top of the page as a sponsored advert. There is also the option of getting your book shown as a suggested product, which will appear on pages when customers are browsing other products in categories that are relevant to your book. You can use keywords to make your book appear visible to those browsing pages relevant to the keywords you have chosen. For more in-depth information about how to use Amazon adverts, go on the websites listed below:

https://kdp.amazon.com/en_US/help/topic/G201499010
https://advertising.amazon.com/resources/library

## Amazon Associates

Being an Amazon Associate allows you to get paid more money from Amazon when selling your book. It's free to be an Amazon Associate. The main benefit of being an Amazon Associate, is that you will get paid every time someone clicks on your associate link to buy your book. You must generate a unique associate link by logging into your Amazon Associates account. Once you have your unique associate link, share that link to the people you want to purchase your book. You can check how many people have purchased your book via your associate link by logging into your Amazon Associates account.

The great thing about being an Amazon Associate; is that you receive commission not only on the book you sell, but also on the sale of any items which are purchased on Amazon within a 24-hour timeframe of someone opening the associate link you sent them. For example, someone buys your book using your associate link. An hour later, that person goes back on Amazon and buys; a book by another author, some headphones, and a camera. In this case, you will get paid commission for all those items that the person purchased.

In order to get paid commission from Amazon Associates at the end of the month, you have to reach their minimum payout amount for them to disburse funds. If you haven't reached the minimum payout amount, Amazon will keep hold of your money until funds in your account have reached the minimum payout amount.

## Flash Sale

To encourage people to buy your book, you can reduce your book's price for a limited time. A flash sale creates a sense of urgency and scarcity, which can lead to impulse buying because people don't want to miss out on a good deal. The benefit for the customer who buys your book during a flash sale, is that the customer is getting your book at a reduced cost. During the time your book is on flash sale, your aim is to sell more copies of your book than you would have anticipated selling normally. So, you will be making less profit from selling each individual book. But you should make more total profit from book sales because you're selling a higher volume of books.

When doing a flash sale, it's important that people are aware you have a sale going on. This is because it can be the difference as to whether someone buys your book or not. A flash sale gives you a good excuse to do additional promotions of your book. You may know a person or people who are interested in your book but haven't ordered a copy yet. If you don't remind someone about buying your book, they may forget to purchase it or no longer want to buy your book. So, use your flash sale as a way to remind and prompt people into buying your book. Flash sales can be a good promotion strategy because they encourage people to take action to buy your book within a certain period of time.

Some authors sell their book on flash sale via Amazon as a strategy, hoping that their book will become a bestseller because they want the credibility of being able to say their book has been a No. 1 bestseller. On Amazon, you have to sell a certain number of books within a certain period of time to become a bestseller. Some authors set their Kindle (eBook) price as low as 99p. There are authors who even go as far as making their eBook available for free. Authors do that to get more people to buy their eBook, which will help them become a No. 1 bestseller if they get enough sales. Most authors will only manage to get their book No. 1 for a short period of time — hours, a day, or a few days. But that is all they need to be able to call their book a No. 1 bestseller.

# Reviews

Book reviews are very important because they help build credibility of your book. When browsing for your book, people are more likely to buy the book if they see good reviews. Bad reviews can damage the reputation of your book. Get as many people to leave positive book reviews as possible. A common mistake with many authors, is that they get a lot of great feedback about their book verbally or via messages, but they don't get many reviews on the website their book is selling on (usually Amazon). This is often because those authors aren't asking enough of their readers to leave a book review.

Prompt your readers to leave reviews of your book and be persistent with collecting book reviews. You may need to remind some of your readers on more than one occasion to leave a review of your book. Send your readers the link to the website where they can go to write the review. They are more likely to write a review if you send them the link to go to because you have simplified the process by making the website destination available to them in one-click. Your readers may have many things on their minds and they can easily forget about leaving your book review. Therefore, you want to make it as simple as possible for them to leave you a book review.

Another importance of reviews, is that you can use them as testimonials. This is especially useful when posting about your book on social media. It's good to have testimonials and statements from your readers because their viewpoint is neutral. Most authors will say they have written a great book, even if they have written a book which is poor. For that reason, an independent review or testimony of your book from a reader is more credible because it's unbiased.

In regards to leaving reviews on Amazon, even if someone buys your book directly from you or through another channel, they can still leave a review of your book. Sometimes people will be ineligible to post a review on Amazon. This is because they don't have an Amazon account or because they haven't purchased any items on Amazon within a certain period of time that would qualify them to be able to leave a review of a product on Amazon. If someone is unable to leave a review of your book on

Amazon, ask them to leave a review of your book on another website where your book is being sold. If they are unable to leave a review of your book on another website, you can request that they post a review of your book on their social media profile (Facebook, Instagram, etc.). Their followers on social media will see that review/post and that could lead to sales of your book.

# BUILDING A STRONG MEDIA PRESENCE

Build your brand as an author; so that when people think of you, the first thing that comes to their mind is that you're an author. One of the ways you can do this, is by creating a digital identity by adding **Author** to your display name on social media platforms. There will be some people who come across your profile, that will be interested in finding out information about the book you have written. This could lead to sales of you book or someone contacting you about participating in a speaking engagement.

Maintain a digital identity in people's minds by regularly posting pictures, videos, and other information promoting your book on your social media accounts. It's good to give people viewing the post, something that gives them an insight into the book. Then, follow that up by stating that they can find out more information about the topic mentioned in your post by reading your book, and then include a link to where your book can be purchased.

Join Facebook groups which are relevant to the topic of your book. These groups should also have a large number of followers and a high level of engagement from group members. When making posts about your book in these Facebook groups, create posts about your book that adds valuable information and is relevant to the group you are posting in.

## Examples

- If you have written a book about fitness and you are going to post in a fitness group, you could state five ways to stay fit that you mentioned in your book.

- If you have written a book on dating and you are going to post in a dating group, then you could do a post which has relationship advice or tips.

- If you have written a book on cooking and you are going to post in a food group, then you could do a post about one of the dishes that you included in your book.

- If you have written a book about mental health and you are going to post in a mental health group or general wellbeing group, you could post something informative about mental health.

My debut book, *The Rise of Rastafari*, is about Rastafari. I have joined several Rastafari groups on Facebook. There are dates throughout the year that Rastafarians celebrate. During those important dates for Rastas, I post information in various Rastafari groups about the importance of those dates. I always state in those posts that people can find out more information about the topic by purchasing a copy of my book, and I include a link to where people can buy my book from.

## Facebook

Create a Facebook page for your book and build a following by inviting people to like your page. Post regular content about your book and add pictures of your book such as the front cover, pictures of people holding your book, and pictures from events. Post information about upcoming events you will be participating in. Also, post book reviews and include the website link to where your book can be purchased from.

Facebook Ads is a marketing campaign that allows you to boost a post or page likes, based on your selection from the options Facebook provides. You set a period of days to run the marketing campaign and you set a daily budget. Facebook Ads allows you to select your target audience by using keywords and choosing their location and age. Facebook Ads also has an option to allow you to promote your post to audiences on Instagram as well as on Facebook.

## Facebook and Instagram

Instagram is another very popular social media platform which you can use to promote your book. Find different angles to promote your book rather than repeating the same posts frequently.

Below, there are bullet points with a list of different ways of how you can promote your book on your Facebook and Instagram profile pages.

- Post photos of your book such as customers holding your book or pictures from events.
- Post details about your upcoming events.
- Post book reviews.
- Share videos and audio of you speaking about your book.
- Message your contacts using either the direct or indirect sales approach.

- Get your contacts to post about your book on their profile.
- Talk about your book on Facebook Live and Instagram Live.

## WhatsApp

Share content promoting your book to your contacts via WhatsApp. Also, share content promoting your book in your WhatsApp groups. WhatsApp allows you to broadcast a single message to all the contacts you have selected. Share different promotional content about your book to your WhatsApp contacts and to those in the same WhatsApp groups as you.

## Clubhouse

Clubhouse is a social media app where people can communicate via meetings. These meetings are called "rooms" on Clubhouse. Rooms are usually open to the public unless the host of a group has chosen to limit the room attendees to only members of their group. In the rooms, you will be able to hear and communicate via audio; people won't be able to see you via video but you are able to add a profile picture. Clubhouse has been designed to be used on smartphones and tablet devices. If you don't have Clubhouse installed on your phone or tablet, you can download Clubhouse for free via the Apple Store or the Google Play Store. You will need Wi-Fi or mobile data to use the app. Once you have installed Clubhouse on your phone, go on the app and create your profile. When you create a Clubhouse profile, put information in your profile such as: the title of your book, a link to where your book is available, your social media links, and your contact information.

After you have created your Clubhouse profile; search for groups which are for authors, writers, and groups focused on topics which are relevant to your book. Join some of those groups and you will receive notifications when those groups are having an event. On the Clubhouse home screen, it will also show you if there is a room taking place which is being held by a group that you are a member of. You can also set a reminder for a specific event or for an event hosted by a specific person. By doing that, you will get a notification on your phone before the event you have chosen to be reminded about is scheduled. There is also an option to receive notifications of events via Outlook calendar. Many of the events on Clubhouse are recorded. So, you can listen to the replay if you weren't able to attend an event.

There are daily rooms for authors on Clubhouse. In some of the rooms; attendees are given the opportunity to speak about their book for a short period. If you contact the organiser of a group in advance regarding promoting your book, the organiser may allow you to promote your book in their room for a longer period of time. I have come across several groups where organisers collaborate with authors to do rooms focused on promoting specific authors. I have even seen group organisers collaborate with authors to do book launches on Clubhouse.

Clubhouse allows you to network with people inside and outside of meetings. If you need to have a one-to-one conversation with someone, you can create a separate room between you and them or you can message each other privately. Clubhouse is a good app to use because it can give you more exposure and it gives you the opportunity to create a bigger network. As a result of that, you can increase your book sales, raise awareness of your book amongst people who would never have come across your book otherwise, and potentially be invited to other speaking engagements to promote your book.

Clubhouse is also a good place to go for learning because there are many rooms for authors where fellow authors share marketing and sales advice and tips. Therefore, you can gain valuable information which can help you to market and sell your book. As Clubhouse is an international platform, there are people you can connect with who are in different countries.

## Recordings

It's important to keep recordings of your speaking engagements because they will come in handy when marketing your book to people later on to reach a bigger audience than people who just attended the event or listened to the live radio show. When I was living in Gambia, I did an educational lecture in one of the schools about my debut book, *The Rise of Rastafari*. There were up to 100 students who I delivered the lecture to. The students loved the lecture, but I didn't sell any books to anyone. However, the lecture was recorded and shared on a popular YouTube channel. I also uploaded the video on my YouTube channel. The video has had over 8,600 views worldwide (combined total of views from both YouTube channels). And that video has led to sales of my book.

# Podcasts

Creating your own podcast can be a great way to build a following. Podcasts are becoming very popular. The great thing about podcasts, is that people can listen to them on demand. There are plenty of platforms where you can host your podcasts. These platforms include: YouTube, Spotify, Anchor, Podomatic, Audible, iTunes, Apple Podcasts, Mixcloud, and Amazon Music. You could do a podcast series where you talk about a different chapter of your book on each episode. For example: Episode 1 (Chapter 1), Episode 2 (Chapter 2), Episode 3 (Chapter 3), and so on. You could create podcast episodes around specific topics or themes which are mentioned in your book. If you already have a podcast, advertise your book on your podcast to your listeners.

# YouTube channel

Create a YouTube channel and start posting content relating to your book on your YouTube channel. Your YouTube channel should have different interviews and talks you have done. For each video you upload, include links to where people can purchase your book in the video description and comments section. When you upload new content on YouTube, share the videos within your social media networks. Someone may watch your YouTube video and decide to buy a copy of your book. Build a following on YouTube by getting people to subscribe to your channel. Your subscribers will receive notifications when you have uploaded another video on YouTube.

## Video Editing Software

To make your videos look more professional than the raw video footage, you can get your videos edited before you upload them. You can edit the videos yourself or get someone to edit your videos for you. If you hire a professional video editor, they'll use a video editing software that they are familiar with. If you are doing the video editing, you will need to choose a video editing software to use. There are a variety of video editing software's that you can buy online. I use Wondershare Filmora Pro when I need to edit my videos. I recommend Wondershare Filmora Pro because it's easier to use than many other professional video editing software.

Adobe Premiere is commonly used by professional video editors (especially those in the media industry). However, Adobe Premiere is for more advanced video editors. Beginners will likely struggle with using Adobe Premiere unless they have undergone training on how to use it. Final Cut Pro is also a good software and it is user friendly, but it is only available on Apple computers. Video editing can take hours or days, depending on the editing needed and the resolution of the video file. If you want it done to a good standard, it requires a skillful person to do it. You can learn to video edit yourself, but it can be very time-consuming and you may still struggle with video editing.

You may want to upload some videos that haven't been edited and some videos that have been edited. The benefit of having your video professionally edited is that the video editor can add: text, branding, backgrounds, pictures, video clips, video transitions, and special effects. A video editor can cut out parts of the video footage which you don't want to keep. And, a video editor can adjust the colour and volume of your video if necessary. But don't expect the video editor to do miracles; you still need to record your video in a well-lit area, with little background noise.

The cost is the main disadvantage of getting a professional video editor, especially considering you could spend money on having your video edited and not make any sales. Prices can vary depending on the job needed to be done and the level of experience of the video editor. I offer video editing services, send an email to makonnensankofa@hotmail.com for prices. You can hire a video editor from websites such as fiverr.com or upwork.com.

## Influencer

You may know a celebrity, an influencer, or someone with a large number of followers who can help promote your book. Having an influencer to endorse your product; can help increase your book sales, especially if your influencer is recognised as an authority amongst the audience who you are trying to sell your book to. **Example:** I was able to get my book, *The Rise of Rastafari*, promoted on social media by the editor of *Jus Jah Magazine*. My book is targeted at Rastafarians and people who are interested in Rastafari. *Jus Jah Magazine* have tens of thousands of international followers on their social media platforms. As a result of my book promotion from *Jus Jah Magazine*, I saw a significant increase in sales of my book that week.

I had an interview about my second book, *Life in Gambia,* which was uploaded onto *Blaxit* YouTube channel. The CEO and presenter of *Blaxit* is Juliet Ryan, who is seen as a big influencer on YouTube by her audience. *Blaxit* is a popular YouTube channel with around 60,000 subscribers. The channel is about encouraging people of African heritage living in the diaspora to relocate to Gambia. My book, *Life in Gambia*, is about my experience of relocating to Gambia as someone of African heritage born in the diaspora. It was ideal for me to speak about my book on *Blaxit* because the audience who watch the channel, are the same audience who my book is aimed at. My interview on *Blaxit* has had almost 2,500 views. Juliet endorsing my book on *Blaxit*, is an example of how I was able to get an influencer to help me with my book promotion by raising awareness of my book to my target audience.

When looking for speaking engagements, look for people, television channels, YouTube channels, radio stations, and organisations that show content relevant to the subject matter of the book you have written. Then, contact them with a proposal requesting to go on their platform. I managed to get an interview on *I Never Knew TV*, which is a popular YouTube channel that has over 250,000 subscribers. On that channel, they feature a lot of content about Rastafari and reggae music artists. So, I thought *I Never Knew TV* would be an ideal place for me to promote my book, *The Rise of Rastafari*, because my book is about Rastafari and there is a chapter in my book which is specifically about the connection between Rastafari and reggae. Another reason why I wanted to feature on *I Never Knew TV*, was to get exposure from their large international audience (subscribers).

I initially contacted *I Never Knew TV* via email. I sent them a message about featuring on their channel, along with the summary of my book and a breakdown of the different chapters included in my book. A few days later, I received a reply from *I Never Knew TV*. They invited me to be interviewed on their YouTube channel. We arranged an interview and they put a short video of my interview on their YouTube channel. The video has been very popular; it has had over 46,000 views. *I Never Knew TV* uploaded the audio of my full interview as a podcast on their website. They also advertised my book on their website and Instagram page.

As a result of my interview and my book promotion from *I Never Knew TV*, I got many book sales. My experience with *I Never Knew*

*TV*, is a prime example of the importance of being proactive in seeking opportunities that will help increase your sales. That's because if I hadn't contacted *I Never Knew TV* and asked for them to interview me, I wouldn't have gotten that opportunity which led to a big increase in my book sales. In some cases, you may need to pay an influencer to promote your book. In this case, you should weigh up whether you think you will make enough profit back from your investment and then make a decision.

# THE INTERNATIONAL MARKET

Many authors limit their market to a local or national market rather than the international market. As an author, you should try to get as many people to read your book as possible. You may have a book which has a niche market and only a small percentage of people in your country are interested in that particular topic. Therefore, you should market your book to people internationally because you will have a much bigger target market.

For example: people of African heritage are the target market for my book, The Rise of Rastafari. However, there is a very small percentage of people of African heritage living in England, which is the country I lived in and the place where I released my book. So, instead of only targeting my book at people of African heritage living in England; I market my book internationally because there are billions of people of African heritage around the world.

With my second book, *Life in Gambia*, I targeted the book at descendants of enslaved Africans who were born in the diaspora. I market that book internationally because there are descendants of enslaved Africans across the world who are interested in finding out more about their African heritage and/or planning to relocate to an African country, especially those in the U.S (United States). The number of descendants of enslaved Africans who are relocating to Africa from the U.S is higher than those relocating to Africa from any other country in the world. The U.S has the second biggest population of descendants of enslaved Africans, and African-Americans in the U.S (as a group) earn more money than people of African heritage who live in any other country around the world.

If you want to maximise international book sales, it's important that you market your book to people in countries where most of the people can afford to buy books and there is a general interest in reading among the people living in those countries. If you're a British author, the U.S market is a good international market to enter because the U.S has a large population of people who have a high amount of disposable income, and it's common for people to read books in the U.S.

Another benefit of targeting people in the U.S, is that there are millions of people living there who have moved from all over the world.

You may have a book that would appeal to people from a specific country/background, but the majority of people in that country live on a low income and cannot afford to buy a book. Diasporans from that low-income country who are living in the U.S, will be able to purchase the book because they have more disposable income.

For people in the U.S looking for places outside the country to market your book, I would suggest countries such as Canada or England because they are countries with big populations, people living in those countries have high disposable incomes, and reading books is very common in those countries. I also suggest Canada and England because those are English-speaking countries, so you don't need the book to be written in another language for people to be able to read the book. Of course, your target market will still depend on the book you have written. But you will miss out on the opportunity to sell your book to a higher volume of people if your target audience are only people who live in the same country as you.

If you go on holiday or move to another country, take your books abroad with you so you can raise awareness of your book in that country. If your book is self-published, you could even get copies printed abroad if you need extra copies. During your time abroad, try to get your books stocked in bookstores. If you've moved abroad or you are going to be abroad for a long time, you should look for speaking engagement opportunities and events where you can market and sell your book.

Whilst your abroad, network and build connections with people. Talk about your book to people; whether that be at the hotel, the beaches, meeting locals, expat meet-ups, or other gatherings. If people don't know you have written a book, they can't buy it from you. The more people that know you're an author and that you have written a book, the more likely it is that your book sales will increase. Capture pictures and videos of you at events and other places, so you can share them on your social media accounts.

Travelling abroad is a great opportunity for you to promote your book internationally. However, you can still be successful at selling books around the world whether or not you travel abroad. Don't worry if you're unable to travel to other countries to promote your book, because you can communicate with people all over the world at the touch of a button via social media. Build an international following on social media and be in groups with people who live in different countries.

# COLD CALLING

Cold calling is a type of marketing which involves contacting a potential customer or client who has not expressed previous interest in speaking with a customer service representative or making a purchase. Cold calling is often carried out through door-to-door knocking, phone calls, and approaching people in the street. Although many people don't like to do jobs that involve cold calling, a lot of businesses do some form of cold calling to help generate sales. As an individual, you can do cold calling to sell copies of your book. If you master cold calling, you could see a big increase in your book sales. You can spend as much or as little time as you want to on doing cold calling. There are people who sell copies of their book full-time by cold calling. Whilst others only do cold calling in their spare time.

In this section, I will be referring to the type of cold calling which involves approaching potential customers in the street. Cities with town centres are good areas to do cold calling because they are places that have a high footfall of people, and most people in town centres have disposable income. So, you are likely to meet people who are shopping or working in those areas. Busy high streets are also good areas to cold call. If you are shy or anxious about doing cold calling, you may want to build up your confidence by beginning cold calling in a quiet location or an area you feel comfortable with. A benefit of cold calling in public, is that your location is flexible. You can do cold calling in other towns, other cities, and other countries.

Cold calling is a numbers game; you should aim to talk to as many people as possible. Not everyone will buy from you but the more people you speak to, the more sales you will get. To be successful with cold calling, you need to have a positive mindset. Otherwise, you probably won't make sales. Be sure to maintain good body language and a normal voice tone when you are speaking to potential customers. Remember, the energy you give out will be the energy you get back. If your body language or your tone of voice is off, people will pick up on that and they will be less likely to buy a copy of your book.

Check the surroundings of the area you are in and be observant about what's going on because there could be something around you or something happening which you can use as a way to *break the ice* and start a conversation with someone passing by. You may want to approach people by saying something light-hearted or humorous as an opener. This can put the people you are approaching in a more relaxed mood and it can make them feel more comfortable about engaging in a conversation with you.

It's essential that you are passionate about what you are selling and that you give potential customers a reason to buy your book by telling them why your book is unique and how it may benefit them. On some occasions, you won't sell copies of your book, but you'll have had good interactions with potential customers. Those positive interactions should boost your morale, give you some confidence, and encourage you to keep going. After you have a good interaction or sale, your morale will be boosted. Take that positive morale into the next conversation you have.

To be successful with cold calling, you need to be able to identify the right people to spend time with and be able to close the sale when the opportunity arises. You should be observant about the people you talk to. Assess their body language and how invested they are in the conversation. If they have given you the right signals, escalate to closing the sale. A good indication to close the sale, is if you are talking to someone and they are listening to you attentively and making comments or asking you questions about your book.

Don't try to sell your book to people who are giving you negative signals because it will dampen your spirit, frustrate you, and make you feel like you're wasting your time doing cold calling (especially during the early stages of cold calling). Always remember, you are a cold caller and not a beggar. Your responsible for choosing the people you want to sell your book to. Have the mentality that you are selling a valuable product and that the person who doesn't buy your book, is missing out on something very important. Also, have an abundance mentality with the mindset that it's no big deal if one person doesn't buy from you because someone else will.

To be successful with cold calling, you need to be persistent. You may need to speak to a lot of people before you sell a copy of your book. But if you have good conversational skills and know when to close the sale, it's likely you will make sales within a shorter period of time. Remember, every no means your one step closer to a yes. Once you have mastered cold calling; you will find it easier to convert sales from potential customers. You will even be able to persuade some people from not buying your book to buying your book.

**Disclaimer:** Cold calling should not be carried out by those who are: under adult age, elderly, disabled, mentally ill, or otherwise vulnerable. Authors who take part in cold calling, should exercise caution and use their own negligence and intuition when deciding on the individuals whom they choose to approach and interact with.

# OTHER USEFUL TIPS

- Sign up for a marketing course to get tips and advice on how to market your book. There are many book coaches who offer marketing services to help authors with marketing their books. I offer one-on-one marketing sessions. For enquires and bookings to do with the marketing sessions I offer, send me an email: makonnensankofa@hotmail.com

- Giveaway a digital chapter of your book for free. Then follow-up with the reader to get feedback from them. If they liked reading the free chapter of your book, ask them if they would like to buy the book so they can read the rest of the chapters.

- Set targets for how many books you expect to sell each month. Having targets should make you try harder to get sales. Even if you don't hit your target, you may achieve more sales than you would have made if you hadn't set a target. That's because by having a target, you're aiming towards something as opposed to having no aim. When setting targets, make sure the targets you set are realistic.

- Publish a revised edition of your book. By doing this, it gives you a new angle to market your book. Customers who bought the first edition of your book, may buy the revised edition if they liked reading the original edition. For people who haven't already got your book, a revised edition gives them another reason why they should buy your book. This is because the revised edition has new content which isn't included in your first book (e.g., a new chapter).

- When you write a new book, include an advertisement of your previous book(s). The reason for this, is that people who enjoyed reading your latest book, may want to buy another book you have written, especially if the book is part of the same series or on a similar topic. You will see that on two pages at the back of this book, there are adverts of my previous books. Hopefully, you buy those books too!

- To encourage people to buy more of your book titles, you could offer promotional pricing for people who purchase two or more of your different books. Example: Let's say one of your books cost £15 and another one of your books cost £13. You could do an offer of two books for £25 to entice people to buy both books from you. Or, you could sell one book at the full price and then give them a discounted price if they buy another one of your books.

# NOTES

_____

_____

_____

_____

_____

_____

_____

_____

_____

_____

_____

_____

_____

_____

_____

_____

_____

_____

_____

_____

_____

_____

_____

_____

_____

_____

_____

_____

_____

_____

_____

_____

_____

_____

_____

_____

_____

_____

_____

_____

_____

_____

_____

_____

_____

_____

_____

_____

_____

_____

_____

_____

_____

_____

_____

_____

_____

_____

_____

_____

_____

_____

_____

_____

_____

_____

_____

_____

_____

_____

_____

_____

_____

_____

_____

_____

_____

_____

_____

_____

_____

_____

_____

_____

_____

_____

_____

_____

_____

_____

_____

_____

_____

_____

_____

_____

_____

_____

_____

_____

# ABOUT THE AUTHOR

Makonnen Sankofa is the founder of The Black Books Show, a best-selling author, a radio show presenter, a public speaker, and a book coach. He is also an experienced sales professional. Makonnen has ten years of experience in the sales industry and has been a top-seller for some of the most established international and national companies. Makonnen currently runs a business that offers media and digital marketing services for authors. His business has helped hundreds of authors from around the world in promoting their books to an international market.

A common thing Makonnen found while running his business, is that many authors are able to publish their books but they struggle with marketing and selling them, particularly new authors. As a result, Makonnen decided to write this book to provide his fellow authors with some tips and advice on how they can increase their book sales by implementing proven sales and marketing techniques that have worked for him and other best-selling authors. This book is aimed at aspiring authors, new authors, and other authors who need help with marketing their book. In addition to new authors, this book can also benefit experienced authors who want to find more ways to maximise their book sales.

In 2019, Makonnen released his debut book called *The Rise of Rastafari: Resistance, Redemption & Repatriation*. He wrote the book to give the reader a clear understanding of what Rastafari is, and to dispel the stereotypes and common misconceptions people have about Rastafari. The book covers crucial information about the origins of Rastafari, the key figures in the movement, the persecution of Rastafari over the years, the influence of Rastafari on reggae music, and the contributions Rastafari has made to the African liberation struggle. A revised edition of *The Rise of Rastafari* was published in 2022.

Makonnen spent six months living in Gambia during 2019. His experiences in Gambia inspired him to write his second book, *Life in Gambia: The Smiling Coast of Africa*. During Makonnen's stay in Gambia; he taught in schools, experienced the Gambian culture, visited local villages, and witnessed several events, including a wedding and three naming ceremonies. He also worked with Juliet Ryan on the popular YouTube channel, *Blaxit*, which reached 20,000 subscribers in the first three months of launching and had an average of 10,000 views per video uploaded. *Blaxit* has helped hundreds of descendants of enslaved Africans in the diaspora to relocate to Africa.

In May 2020, Makonnen founded The Black Books Show (known then as The Black Books Webinar). Each month, authors of African heritage speak about their books on his platform. The event showcases international authors who have written books on different topics including: history, culture, health, fitness, domestic violence, societal issues, children's books, cooking, romance, sicknesses, and more. The Black Books Show has featured over 200 authors of African heritage from around the world.

In June 2021, Makonnen expanded The Black Books Show by launching a bi-weekly radio show on two stations. During the radio shows, Makonnen conducts in-depth interviews with authors of African heritage. After the show is broadcasted, he makes the show available on-demand as a podcast. Makonnen also offers book coaching courses for aspiring authors who want to learn how to publish a book, as well as coaching courses for authors who need help marketing their book.

# CONNECT WITH AUTHOR MAKONEN SANKOFA

If you liked reading *How to Market and Sell Your Book*, please leave a review on Amazon. You can leave a review on Amazon regardless of where you bought the book. Also, please recommend the book to other aspiring authors or authors who need help with marketing and selling their books.

**Stay Connected**

Facebook: Makonnen Sankofa

Instagram: @makonnen.sankofa

YouTube channel: Makonnen Sankofa

Email: makonnensankofa@hotmail.com

For bookings and enquiries regarding marketing courses by Makonnen Sankofa, please send a message to the email address provided above.

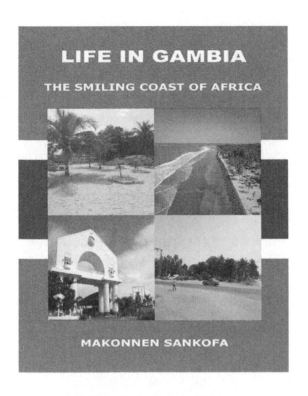

## Life in Gambia:
## The Smiling Coast of Africa

## Makonnen Sankofa

## Available to buy on Amazon
## (Paperback and Kindle)

## Order your copy today!

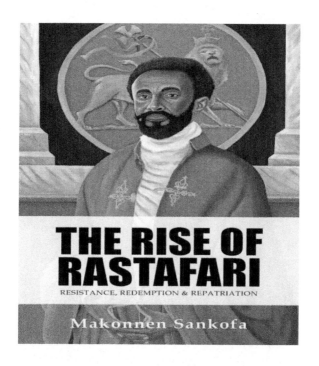

## The Rise of Rastafari: Resistance, Redemption & Repatriation

## Makonnen Sankofa

## Available to buy on Amazon (Paperback and Kindle)

## Order your copy today!

Printed in Great Britain
by Amazon